THE NIGHT GARDEN

Of My Mother

A Memoir

Sandra Tyler

Author of

BLUE GLASS

A New York Times
Notable Book of the Year

Praise for BLUE GLASS

LOVELY AND UNUSUAL...Of all the novel's virtues, this is perhaps the rarest: an evenhanded understanding that illuminates both the particularity of the relationship and the universality of mother-and-daughter conflicts.

Jane Smiley
The New York Times Book Review

THE AUTHOR DOES AN OUTSTANDING JOB of keeping the reader in suspense as to how it will all turn out; A good look at the quiet–and not-so-quiet–rebelliousness felt by every teenager. Recommended for all fiction collections, and possibly some older YA collections.

Library Journal

AN UNPRETENTIOUS BUT ACCOMPLISHED FIRST NOVEL about the bittersweet relationship between a mother and a daughter... one of those quietly compelling stories that touches the heart.

Kirkus Reviews

THIS STRONG, THOUGHTFUL FIRST NOVEL about a young girl and her changing relationship with her parents develops with quiet momentum beneath its cool, unadorned surface.

Publisher's Weekly

Praise for AFTER LYDIA

IN THIS EMOTIONALLY ACUTE NOVEL, Tyler questions whether family members ever truly know one another. Tyler's drama, loaded with screenplay-friendly dialogue, proceeds smartly and stingingly.

Publisher's Weekly

SANDRA TYLER'S MOODY SECOND NOVEL takes place a year after the title character is killed while crossing the railroad tracks in a small coastal town in Massachusetts... Ms. Tyler is best at revealing the habitual role playing and fault lines beneath the everyday banter.

Scott Veal, *The New York Times*

THIS WRITING IS CAREFUL, EVEN GRACEFUL, DANCING off, slantwise, the grief that dwells with us in our dwellings... Anybody that can curl up in a chair and read past dusk should find this book and take it home. Anybody who has a child, who has a parent, who has taken turns in their life that might have been mistakes, that disguise the wished for, the abandoned, the great fear of the dark, should take this book home and enjoy it.

Anne Roiphe, *The East Hampton Star*

Praise for THE NIGHT GARDEN

A RICH AND POIGNANT ACCOUNT of a daughter's complex relationship with her aging mother and the emotional toll of illness, loss, and love.

Maryanne O'Hara
Author of LITTLE MATCHES: A MEMOIR
OF FINDING LIGHT IN THE DARK

THE NIGHT GARDEN IS HONEST IN A HARD-WON, bracing way. Readers will value it for that. Ours remains a society of denial and here is an unrelenting portrait of love and loss, step by step, humbling detail by detail, in a prose that has transcended self-pity and pain and won its lived perspective.

DeWitt Henry, Founder of *Ploughshares*
Author of **The Marriage of Anna Maye Potts**
and **Trim Reckonings**

THE NIGHT GARDEN

Of My Mother

Copyright © 2024 • All Rights Reserved
Pierian Springs Press
Sandra Tyler

Other than review quotes or academic excerpts,
no part of this work may be reproduced
without explicit permission.

First printing, October 2024
Library of Congress Control Number: 2024936825
ISBN 978-1-953136-77-0 Hardback
ISBN 978-1-953136-76-3 Paperback
ISBN 978-1-953136-78-7 Audiobook

Cover Design by Kurt Lovelace
Cover Artwork by Pierian Springs Press
Cover type *Bauhaus Dessau* **Alfarn** by Céline Hurka,
Elia Preuss, Flavia Zimbardi,
Hidetaka Yamasaki, and Luca Pellegrini.
Body & Chapter Titles set in **Nimbus**
Chapter dropcaps set in **Mrs Eaves XL**
Headers in **Jenson** by Robert Slimbach
Flourishes set in Emigre Foundry **Dalliance**, by Frank Heine &
Emigre Foundry **ZeitGuys**, by Bob Aufuldish, Eric Donelan.
Typefaces licensed Adobe, Linotype, Emigre, & URW GmbH.

PSPress.Pub
Pierian Springs Press, Inc
30 N Gould St, Ste 25398
Sheridan, Wyoming 82801-6317

For
My Mother

You have left me a white moon scrubbed across an unfinished canvas. But when I look up, I still hear you: "Oh, Sandy, just *look* at that s*ky!*"

PROLOGUE

I remember it this way: my whole self sprawled across her, my mother's body.

Because *no*. I wouldn't let them take her—those funereal men, looking absurd in starched suits standing there in my mother's weedy gravel driveway, nervously pulling on their cuffs *because the crazed daughter wouldn't let them take her mother*. I don't remember their faces, only their vehicles, the black van that would take away my mother, the other, a pristine white escort car; for show. For me. Their audience.

I peered at them through my mother's dusty Venetian blinds.

No.

I let the slat drop.

I pulled out loose strands of her white hair. I thought about getting up for a pair of scissors, to clip some, to keep once my mother's body was reduced to ash. But that would mean getting up, leaving this moment. Leaving my mother.

I splayed her fingers, studied the plastic fake-gem ring my son had bought for her at the school fair. The one I would insist she be cremated wearing, I'm not sure why. Maybe because when I'd prepaid for the cremation, I was baffled by the funeral director assuring me the cremains "would be all bone, no teddy bears."

Her circulation having ceased, my mother's fingers seemed bloodless, translucent. *Beautiful* in their translucency. Stunning in their stillness—only yesterday, they'd been flitting about, feeling for the edge of her fleece throw, reaching up to explore her own face as if an object she did not recognize. Since her stroke, she'd lost so much body mass, her hands were transformed. From the tough knobbiness of the arthritic to the fragile. Literally breakable; when she was rotated regularly to avoid bedsores, one hand might get caught beneath her hip, and her aide was quick to free it: "We can't have *that* happen."

No.

We can't have that happen.

Because now her hands were as delicately boned as a bird's. As the sparrow's, the one flitting about our porch back home, where I sat most nights, with a bottle of wine. Flitting about like my mother's hands, searchingly, failing to find a place to settle, and I'd long to cup the panicked bird. The sparrow would fly off, into our bushes, into the dark, leaving a wake of trembling leaves, and I'd down a diazepam with the last of the wine; my doctor, noting my distress, had raised the dose from 5 to 10 mg, but in that last year, on nights after my mother was back in emergency, after her stroke, and when she no longer could place me in time, sometimes I slipped another pill.

Now as my mother lay dead, I was both moved and horrified by the fact that I actually found beauty in her hands. Horrified because it wrenched me to see my once strong mother, even in death, reduced to the easily snapped of delicate bones. But moved by the secrets of her hands: the intricacy of veins branching out into that translucency, the strident blue of an early evening sky, into those last traces of light.

My mother's aide came in. The men in starched suits were threatening to leave. *Without the body.*

I clung to my mother as I hadn't been able to do when she was alive. When the slightest touch caused her pain.

Nooooooo!

I remember that, my wailing. Hearing it from a distance, the way we could hear the ocean from her deck, when we used to sit out there in the summer. That thunderous breaking of the waves on a still night.

It didn't make *sense* to take my mother from her own house. "This is *her house*!" I cried out, into my mother's room. Into the April morning, its cruel brightness slicing though those blinds, across me and my dead mother in the hospital bed....

The hospital bed. A glacial presence in the midst of the familiar—of the fragile antique rocking chair cracked from too many nurses sitting on it to fill out their charts; lining her bookshelf, the brittle starfish and broken shells my mother had collected along the beach; my mother's desk, the letter slots packed with all my old sentimental Valentines, birthday and Mother's Day cards; yellowed cat notepads; loose photos of me, a toddler pulling up dandelions; of her, helping me to dress my Barbie in a red skirt she crocheted; then the black-and-white when she was my age now, in her fifties: she's sitting in a chair, turning all her attention to me, to my showing her some lopsided dish I'd made, reaching for it. The way she'd always turned her attention to me. The way we'd always been, resurrected months later, when more things of our lives together resurfaced: more loose photographs I'd come across cleaning out her bureau drawers, tucked in with her necklaces kept carefully untangled in their separate boxes. I would find them mixed in with old board games in the living-room chest, falling out from old cookbooks. My mother was an artist, and I'd find her sketchbooks filled with drawings of all the places we'd travelled to together, side streets in Florence, the old adobe churches in New Mexico. Then drawings going back to our beginning, of me in my high chair, on a rocking horse, playing with the cord phone. I'd find my own drawings, preserved in wood frames she'd painted herself, or pressed between cardboard so that only their edges had yellowed.

My mother's aide, the who persevered through so many others who were fired, quit, or left for the more lucrative of managerial office jobs, was standing over me. Over us. Quietly pleading, trying to keep her voice even so as not to annoy the crazy-grief-stricken-fifty-two-year-old child clinging to her mother's frail bones. Bones sheathed in loose bruised dehydrated skin.

The child, in the end, relented—she allowed the starched men into her mother's house. Who promised to treat her mother with "the utmost dignity and respect."

"Fuck *you*!" The child screamed. *Spat* the words.

They stood there stunned. Or maybe just politely allowing the awful moment to pass, before slipping the stretcher into my mother's room and shutting the door. It would be weeks later when I would chastise myself for not thinking to dress her, had not thought how they would remove the fleece throw to reveal her in only a Depends and a stained white T-shirt.

In my mother's foyer with her potted plants, I slumped to the floor. Pressed my hands into her cold cracked tiles.

After they'd slipped her mother into the back of the shiny black van, after she watched them drive away with her from her mother's own home, up the street, the sun now cresting the tops of the budding trees, the child climbed back into the hospital bed. Onto the air mattress that inflated and deflated. And cresting each wave, she cried out for her mother, into the still room:

Mommy!
Mommmmyyy!!

PART I

1

That was the last time I ever cried for my mother. I mean, *cried*. The heaving of real tears that shook the hospital bed, left me spent. Otherwise, I only managed a moaning, a grief laboring to erupt after years of my wishing her gone, but wishing she would never leave me—I could not imagine *that*, my life without her, even though our relationship had morphed into something so distorted, I hardly recognized us as the mother and daughter we had always been. And so, entirely unmoored, and to mask the unimaginable that now had become real, nightly after putting our boys to bed, I sat on our porch, staring out at stark trees, trying to make sense of it all, with a bottle of wine capped off with the diazepam; the reason after she died, my primary care physician would send me to psychiatric emergency, where eventually I was admitted, to have taken away not only my phone, but my sweatshirt because I could have hung myself with the drawstrings. Where I would be woken up daily with two questions: had I had a bowel movement in the last 24 hours and was I feeling suicidal? The reason not because I had gone crazy, nor even because I was looking to end my life. But because even after she died, I could not transition back into a normality that long since had stopped seeming normal.

In those final years leading up to my mother's death, there was only the *this*. The immediacy, often real urgency, of the moment, when I'd become a mother myself. A period in both our lives, me now the daughter of a quite elderly mother, I would come to describe as the new normality. A normality defined less by routine than by the disruption of it, when the phone would ring and I'd have to drop what I was doing, turning off a pot of half-cooked spaghetti, leaving it to go undrained and swell for hours, or wet laundry to sour in the washing machine, to drive an hour to meet the ambulance at the hospital.

Most often, these emergency-room scenarios were from her falls, and I would be more angry than afraid—why can't you use your *cane*? Why the *walls*, so you go and fall into your own windows? But I would remember better the extraordinary times: over a lunch of onion soup, when she lost all feeling in her right arm and we thought she was having a stroke from an arterial inclusion. Then shortly before she died, when she actually *was* having a stroke and could not form coherent words on the phone. Those times, a terror seized me, one rooted in me from when once I lost sight of my mother, at age five, up in Vermont where we spent our summers, when she went for a canoe ride across the lake at dusk and receded into the oncoming darkness. *How could I go on without my mother?*

One morning early on in those years, in that final descent into truly old age for my mother, she called when nothing was clearly wrong but something definitely wasn't right.

She was panicked and breathless: "Something's happening."

I was trying to get my boys, then six and seven, off to elementary school. I was finishing up frying some bacon for Owen, the only thing he would eat for breakfast outside of Ramen noodles. I put the cordless phone on speaker, and the receiver on the counter, as I could do—often did—with my mother.

"*What's* happening?"

"Things are all jumbled in my head. I couldn't see for a few minutes..."

"You've had these spells before..."

I gave Owen his plate of bacon and he pointed to the new dog coughing under the kitchen table. "Mom, why's he *doing* that?"

Our new poodle pup had been coughing for a couple of days, like a cat trying to cough up a hairball.

Even if I had an answer as to why our dog was coughing like a cat, I couldn't answer; I was on the phone. With my mother. Who was calling at 7 am as I was then mixing pancake batter for Owen's big brother who would only eat pancakes for breakfast. Or cupcakes. And who hadn't even come downstairs yet. I imagined he was in his room distracted by his new Batmobile.

The dog was coughing, and my mother was calling to tell me she had an irregular heartbeat: "It's all over the place. I've been lying here for two hours waiting for it to go away. I'm afraid to even have coffee. I don't know if I should go to the hospital."

The dog coughed again. "Mom?" Owen was pale with fear, a strip of twisted bacon poised in the air.

"Eat your bacon."

"What?" came my mother's voice from where, I swear, she was rocking the receiver on the counter.

"These spells! They're not *new!*" My excuse for yelling, her hearing shot unless she put her own phone on speaker—which she never would. And there *were* these episodes where her heart would "flutter," ever since her cardiologist had her wear one of those boxes overnight to record her rhythms.

"Not for this *long*," she said irritably. "I'm not ready to die. I don't want to die!"

She said this defensively as if I *wanted* her to die. Which I didn't. Except when I was trying to make a "gazillion" (as Owen liked to exaggerate), breakfasts, on school mornings which usually wound up atypical anyway, with the pup pooping on the hall rug or forgotten backpacks. Well, not die, *just not to call me at 7am.*

Owen went quiet—too quiet, as he was listening too intensely with now big ears.

I picked back up the phone to take it off speaker and moved out into the hall.

Whispering now, I crouched on the stairs: "Then let's call an ambulance."

Lucas now was coming down the stairs, in a pair of too-short pants, and I reminded myself what I would forget, that he needed new clothes. "What's wrong with Gramma?"

"Gramma's having a heart attack," Owen called from the kitchen, as if he knew what that was, as when he'd parrot me about the "ridiculous" cost of a candy bar from 7-Eleven.

Lucas looked at me as horrified as when his first gerbil passed away. "Is she going to die?"

"She's not having a heart attack," I snapped.

"You don't know that!" my mother screeched, directly into my ear.

I didn't know, frankly, whether she was having a heart attack or not. I didn't know a *thing* in those moments. Except that the dog was coughing and *nothing could happen to the dog.*

"Oh, never *mind*," my mother said, as I heard her drop her own cordless onto her bed, her way of hanging up, so that I got to listen to her cussing in the background, about how no one cared whether she lived or died, which only pissed me off and made me yell even louder, until she heard my tiny tinny voice and picked back up the phone.

"What do you *want*?"

"You forgot to press the off button."

"I'm not an *imbecile*..." she said, sounding breathless again, and I was at once devastated and terribly satisfied that I'd almost made her cry.

Then she hung up. This time for real.

In those last years there would be a lot of that—of her hanging up on me. So that we both could simmer at opposite ends of our landlines, as only mothers and daughters can do. Except for times like this when in that cutting of the line, I could feel the distance, the eighty-odd miles between us, as insurmountable.

I served Lucas a burnt hard pancake.

He poked at it. "It's burnt. And *hard*."

"Then starve," I snapped. At a food-allergic child who was afraid of lots of foods and possibly could actually starve if I didn't insist he eat burnt, hard pancakes....

But if I didn't snap, then I was unable to make choices. To rationalize calmly as to what I should do in the next few minutes, when I was being asked to make a choice, and I never knew what or whom to choose.

Instead, I froze. I opened the refrigerator to stare into it for no good reason. At dumbfounded stock-still cartoons of juice and milk.

I called my mother back.

"Hello," she said, pretending as if she wasn't expecting I would do this. Call her back.

"What do you mean you couldn't see?"

She explained about how she had been unable to sleep, so turned on the television—once she could find the remote, which she first thought was the phone—meandering off into some story about how she was lying in bed watching this fascinating show on Antarctica, and there being seven species of Antarctic penguins, one with the "hoot" of a name Macaroni....

I didn't have time for penguins. "*Mom*. Just tell me

what happened."

"Oh, don't be so impatient!"

She told me about how suddenly she just couldn't see the television. Things went blank. "And then things got jumbled. Like things going around and around in my head. Wooden blocks and gears and cogs..."

"Cogs? Are you dizzy?"

"No, I'm not *dizzy* but something's happening. I'm short of breath. I'm feeling nauseous...Oh, I don't feel good..." Now she sounded frightened.

Which made me frightened.

What my mother was finally diagnosed with after countless times over the years of having to wear those heart monitor box things which seemed never to catch the skipped beats, was atrial fibrillation. Which made her higher risk for strokes. Then there was her high blood pressure....

In an instant, my annoyance was whipped up into terror.

"Stay on the phone, Mom." On my cell in my other hand, I called 911.

2

Once again, my mother was headed to the emergency room, and I failed to do what I should do, take a deep breath. Because I failed to take that deep breath, I quickly transmuted into panicked snappy Momma who demanded her boys tie their own sneakers because, after calls to my husband to let him know he may have to pick them up from after-school care, I had more phone calls to make, to arrange for the dog to be walked, and the boys' drop-off at Lucas's best friend's house to catch the bus—and to listen to Owen whine why couldn't *he* go to school with one of *his* friends? At which point, I should have gotten down at eye level with him and asked—oh, ever so *patiently*—do you know what the word *cooperate* means?

Instead I went into manic mode, dumping breakfast bowls and plastic juice glasses into the sink; packing the puppy into his crate, remembering my mother's Big Black Bible, a black binder with thick folders packed with lists of certified home healthcare aides; local community word-of-mouth geriatric do-gooders; phone numbers for her rotating primary care doctors, physical therapist, cardiologist, orthopedist, dentist, dermatologist, ophthalmologist, retina specialist, hand specialist; several copies of her ever-changing list of medications so I could hand them to the nurses who at least, appreciated my daughterly efficiency; my own scribbled notes, frenzied ones, on hospital discharge papers.

Hardly patient to begin with, I could not quell these frenzied moments. I could not do what my therapist advised, to take those deep breaths when I began to have a panic attack and my hands went numb. Instead, I resorted to what I did best, to yell: my *god*, did Owen have to play with his stick magnets *now*, emptying the entire bag onto the carpet? I yanked him up off the floor, and it wouldn't be until that night, the day finally done, when I would see that he had lined the sticks up into neat rows—he'd finally figured out how magnets attract and repel each other. That such perfect alignment could still be achieved.

But as I dropped them off, as the day still loomed ahead, I only felt the weight of my own guilt, about the yelling and the yanking. Once I glimpsed Owen's sad face in my rearview mirror, where he stood in the doorway of his *brother's* best friend's house...all my earlier irritability dissolved into sadness. As it would when I would have to miss his kindergarten Christmas party because of another emergency, and would stop at Target on the way home to grab a pack of glow-in-the-dark stars, as if a cheap solar system could make up for the large hole of my absence.

I blew him a kiss in the mirror, desperate now for him to have a great day; he was going on a field trip to a farm, and I wanted this morning to evaporate into the warm spring air, to be raised up on a light breeze like the white dogwood petals from a nearby tree. I wanted him to be left with this moment, of love and not apologies exactly, but some kind of motherly remorse.

And I was on the road. A route I knew so well, I could predict the bumps in the expressway where I'd have to grip my coffee to keep it from spilling. A stretch of unbroken skyline allowing for no welcomed distractions from my own thoughts so scrambled, they were pureed. I was reduced to a soupy-thoughtless robot gripping a steering wheel, driving that stretch of highway out to my mother's, down from the north shore of Long Island, then east along the coast of the Atlantic Ocean, where the terrain shifted from tall maples to the raw of scrubby pines.

The first time I'd made this trek to the emergency room was when my mother fell and broke her hip, tripping down the brick steps of a restaurant going out to dinner. That time, I got the call from her friend who was riding in the ambulance with her, just as we were finishing our own dinner—I remember vividly the pink of salmon left on our plates; the disarray of our kitchen, Lucas still in a highchair, his own small plastic plate, a bucolic scene of Pooh Bear and Piglet, overturned on his tray; his baby brother at five months, not yet on solid food, bouncing in his bouncy seat.

My husband and I stood at the epicenter of this disarray, trying to figure out what to do. It wasn't as simple as my jumping into the car alone; I was nursing and as a stay-at-home mom, I did not pump. It was quite the dilemma really, as I couldn't bring the baby into emergency, nor could I leave him home for countless hours before I could nurse again. Too short notice to find a sitter, the quickest solution was to pile the whole family into the car—Derek spent the next four hours sitting in the emergency room parking lot while our boys slept in the backseat, except when I'd come out to latch the baby to my engorged breasts.

After that first fall which seemed to predicate all the others, my mother went into rehab, and I visited her daily, leaving the boys with their sitter, coming home only once I was completely engorged. I remember better the excruciating pain of my breasts like tight bags of sharp little rocks, than I do details of this period, I think because it was a truly physical feeling of being torn between my mother's needs and those of my children. A feeling that would become more pronounced as my mother grew more frail, too unstable to help with her grandchildren beyond distracting the baby while safely buckled into his bouncy seat. There's a photograph she took of me when I'd gone out there for a few days: Owen is strapped to my front, Lucas on my hip, while with my one free hand, I am stirring a pot of spaghetti. I am smiling in the photo, but I remember well my feelings in the moment, how they clashed with my mother's of only pure delight. For me, it was quite literally a balancing act—I was already thinking ahead to how exactly I was going to drain the boiling hot water without scalding my baby.

This is a balancing act perhaps not so unusual as more women are having children later in life, when their own parents are on the cusp of elderly. But my mother as well had me later, which back then was unusual—and not entirely acceptable, for a woman of 45 and married to a widow who already had grandchildren, to have a child of her own. And so she'd been a sandwich mom herself, as she too had to be taking care of her elderly mother, already in her 90s, frail and housebound with phlebitis, when I was still only in elementary school. I don't remember what I now know to have been the backdrop to her stalwart determination to fully allow me my childhood—it wasn't until I was grown when I would come to understand the reality of those years for my mother, her juggling of home-care aides and throwing end-of-school parties in our backyard even as my grandmother might have been hospitalized. What I do remember is visiting my grandmother and fanning open a paper dollhouse she kept there for me, and how my grandmother could spin dice across the board when we once played Parcheesi. As I hope my boys only remember the collecting of shells with their grandmother to string into necklaces; her holding the nails while they banged together scraps of wood with a child's hammer in her studio.

Over the course of my mother's life, she became a veteran caregiver, as I suppose were most mothers of that generation. My father was a maritime historian, and she typed his manuscripts for *The Wilke's Expedition*, hundreds of pages and numerous drafts, on his old Royal typewriter. At the same time, she was caring not only for her mother, but for her godmother. I remember how elderly they were when I was still only around age seven, how they'd sit mutely side by side at Christmas dinner, except for the occasional strident screech of their hearing aids. My mother would then host a second Christmas dinner, for my father's son and daughter from his first marriage, and his four grandchildren—I would grow up considering them more cousins than my nieces and nephews, as we were all so close in age. Technically, my mother was a grandmother before she was a mother, and she always felt torn between the two roles, guilty for failing to keep up the photo album of the grandchildren once I was born.

For my mother though, that feeling of being torn really commenced when she was eighteen, when her father had a stroke after he lost everything in the Great Depression, and she began supporting her parents on half her pay check, working in advertising as an art buyer when what she really wanted was to be an artist. She came home every weekend to care for her parents, and after she died, I found drawings of her father slack in large chair, an upward view, and I imagined my mother sitting on the floor, the impatient scratch of her pen. An impatience that would haunt her all of her life, of never having been able to devote herself fully to her art. "Go live your life," she would say to me, not wanting to happen to me what happened to her. "One day I *will* need you."

Like most grown children, I didn't know what my mother "needing" me would exactly entail until my mother wound up more frequently in the emergency room. After she fractured her pelvis, I had to arrange regular childcare so that I could accommodate these needs. I remember being on my cell out in the hall at the hospital, trying to coordinate after-school care for the boys, who were still in preschool. With that fall, she was able to go home and get around, to cobble together her breakfast and microwave her dinners, but I needed to drive out to take her to the grocery store and for follow-up doctor appointments. And so for the next ten years or so, until my mother died, I regularly made that 80-odd mile trek out east, to be with her, stretched in two directions, between two points on a map.

For this emergency, I got caught in rush hour traffic, allotting me too much time to replay various calamitous scenarios, of my mother going into heart failure, or finding her already gone, in one of those pallid cubicles with seafoam green curtains. Worse, that she'd suffered but survived a severe stroke, my mother's own worst scenario: "I can handle anything, but not a *stroke!*" Scenarios replete with telling details of flashing monitor screens, IV needles already set into her right wrist; left one tagged with a red "fall risk" band, her face pale in the dim greenish light.

I found my mother alive, if not entirely well, as the doctors were waiting on results of blood tests, and impatient to leave: "They always rush you so. Everything is, rush, rush, *rush*," she said, recounting how they'd loaded her into the ambulance in just her nightgown. (She also told me that the only good thing about her volunteer crew, was she got the Presbyterian minister again—my mother tended to form crushes on men of the church. She'd come to know all of the volunteer EMS, including the owner of the liquor store where she'd buy her liters of Scotch.)

"I didn't even get to feed the cats." She threw up her hands. "And now we just wait, wait, and *wait.*"

She'd been complaining that she was cold, so I got her a couple of the paper-thin blankets from where I knew they were kept in the warmer by the nurse's desk.

Then she just wanted a comb, wishing she'd had time to at least grab her purse.

I didn't carry a comb, my hair too thick and curly for one, but I rooted through my handbag anyway, grateful for the ordinariness of rummaging through the messy compartments after imagining her dead. I opened a tiny compartment I didn't even know I had.

"How can you not carry a comb?"

I zipped shut all the little compartments in my mammoth bag without another word as I could with my children, when they asked too many questions. There was no cell reception in Emergency, and I could only hope the boys had gotten to school all right. I was already looking forward to escaping out into the cool spring air to check my texts.

Settling into emergency-room-waiting mode, there was just that: nothing to do but wait.

My mother gazed at me across the distance from her bed, to where I sat in a chair whose sea-foam green vinyl matched the curtains. "That new? Your top?" she asked, as she would when she didn't like what I was wearing.

I couldn't help bristling. Though I welcomed the teenage-ish bristling, a feeling far more familiar than the motherly of having to help her put on her shoes as I did with my children.

On our shopping expeditions to T.J. Maxx, she liked to buy me clothes I couldn't envision myself in. Clothes later she wouldn't remember having given me, though she might compliment me on my—finally, *her*—choice of colors.

"*Blue* is becoming on you."

I was wearing salmon pink. A color I knew she did not think "becoming" on me.

"*Phthalo* blue," she said, thinking oil paints, the brilliant blue that often showed up in her paintings. "They have some cute styles out now. I saw something in, I think it was, Soft Surroundings."

I knew she now spent a good part of her days flipping through catalogues, flagging pages with sticky notes, of blue blouses, of miniskirts because she thought I still had the figure: "Doesn't hurt you to show it off a little," she'd been telling me ever since I graduated high school, when she took me shopping before my college freshman year.

"They really have the prettiest things. Maybe for Christmas."

I wasn't in the mood to discuss my wardrobe, never mind Christmas. "It's May."

"Well, I know it's May," she said, tentatively, as if she didn't know.

She rubbed her chin in that way she could when returning to some previous thought. "He even indicated that. How I don't have long. They made me sign a don't revive thing."

"A DNR? That's routine, Mom."

"You don't know that."

I actually *did* know, though decided not to go on about how they probably had her sign the DNR because I was late in getting to them the Health Care Proxy I kept in that Big Black Bible.

But I also knew that she was indeed not dying, having stopped at the nurse's desk for a status. At this particular emergency-room juncture, what I'd discovered about a 92-year-old mother who regularly wound up in Emergency, was that the staff found it all so amusing—the fact that she was still alive and that I was actually concerned for her health. When they paged the doctor, it turned out to be the same one from her last emergency jaunt, when she fell trying to change the litter in the cat's pan; he had reviewed with me old X-rays as we tried to decode the riddle of her fractures, whether this one was new or from a previous fall.

This time he shrugged. "Well, so far it's all rather a mystery."

A *mystery?*

Her vitals were good and EKG normal. But he had ordered a CT scan and blood work to determine whether her enzymes were elevated, which might indicate a heart attack.

"I told you it was my heart," my mother said triumphantly, once I'd settled into her cubicle. "What a CT scan has to do with my heart, I don't know."

"They don't *know* it's your heart, Mom..."

"Of course, it's my heart. What else if not my heart?"

I opted not to suggest that seeing cogs and gears might have to do with her *brain*, thus the CT scan of her head. It was impossible to argue with my mother when she was right. Even when she could be just plain *wrong*.

"Why would he tell me I'm dying if I'm not?" my mother asked.

"*Mom*, you're not—"

"Oh, I know. But I might as well be—I just can't keep up with it all. And my glasses disappearing again...."

"The gremlin."

"You think it's funny. But things do disappear."

"They're probably mixed up in all your papers."

"I know, I'm in such a mess. But there are a lot good reads. I just don't have the time to read them."

This baffled me, how my mother increasingly didn't think she had time, when she had too much time on her hands. It hadn't occurred to me yet that things were taking longer because she couldn't process things as quickly.

"Well, the catalogues then," I said. "Get rid of those at least...." She kept a basket of them by her bed, some so dated, the covers were faded cable-knit sweaters from winters ago.

"But I see things, and I think of the boys—those museum catalogues, what did I see, something I thought of for

Lucas. A kind of puzzle...What about the boys then? What do they want for Christmas?"

"Oh my god, Mom, it's *May*."

"Well, their birthdays then..."

"We just had Owen's, remember? And Lucas's isn't until October."

I don't know why I felt compelled to correct her whenever I felt she was getting confused about time, maybe because, up until she died when she no longer recognized her own home, I could not accept that my mother's mind might actually be going.

My mother went silent then, and I couldn't tell whether she really didn't remember.

But it was a silence I needed to break. "You should see the puppy." I told her about how he could cough like a cat, and she laughed. But then I made the mistake of telling her that it was the first time I'd left him home alone in his crate.

"A crate? Oh, that poor little thing."

"People crate their dogs all the time. That's what it's called, crating. Training them to be alone for a period."

"Oh, how cruel. Why would you train any creature to be *alone*?"

"What did you expect, for me to bring him to the hospital?"

She looked down at her hands.

"He's ok. Alice next door has a key and is going to let him out to walk him."

"I'm sorry I called you."

"Mom, of course you should call me..." I didn't know why I didn't sound more convincing.

"Well, this is silly. It's probably nothing."

"You were seeing cogs and gears."

"I'm 92, Dear, I'm going to see cogs and gears."

I looked down at my own hands, at my ragged nails. I couldn't remember the last time I'd filed them.

"And I left the windows open...the sills will be ruined."

"It's not forecast rain."

"Well, that's not the point. And my poor cats..." she sounded as if about to cry. "Oh, I am sorry. Sorry for it all..."

"Mom." I moved over to sit next to her on the bed.

"Well, you don't need this, with two little ones and a new dog..." She laughed, wiping one eye. "And now your decrepit mother."

I adjusted her nightgown where it was slipping off one shoulder. "You're not decrepit."

She laughed. "You're sweet, Dear, but I am indeed decrepit."

"You're not." Then I laughed. "Not in spirit."

We both laughed. "No. But I am very, very *old*." She pulled herself up a bit. "And now I need to use the John."

When once she used this term in front of the boys, my quizzical youngest thought she was talking about their Uncle John, so we looked up the definition—the original John was a John Harrington who had devised Britain's first flushing toilet.

When she started to move her legs off the bed, I reminded her of the bright red "fall risk" band on her wrist.

"This is ridiculous! I don't want a bedpan."

"And they don't want you walking, Mom. You're all hooked up, anyway."

She looked at the IV snaking from her arm as if just noticing it. She sighed deeply, collapsing back against her pillow, for a moment closing her eyes so that they flickered restlessly beneath her lids. "Oh, why do these things keep happening? Why can't life be a little less eventful?"

I rang the nurse for a bedpan, and while we waited, I pulled out my phone to show her some pictures. As with my children, I'd grown adept at distractions, and I showed her a picture of the new dog.

"Oh, isn't he cunning..." She tapped the screen with a crooked arthritic finger. "And who is that?"

"Mom, it's *Lucas*."

"My *eyes*. I can't see anything anymore." She took the phone to peer at it. "But you know, they are growing. And changing. It's hard to keep up."

As suddenly as I could push her away, I wanted to be close to her, inched myself farther up on the bed. My hand brushed hers. "You're still cold."

She reached up to pat my cheek. "And you're a good daughter."

Scrolling through my photos, I leaned my head against hers, so that we could both peer into the tiny screen.

3

The amusing "mystery" was partially solved by, yes, elevated enzyme levels. But only a two! A very slight elevation, one which indicated some kind of "stress" on the heart, if not an actual heart attack—that subtle difference, still a "mystery" to me. Ordinarily, her doctor would have recommended a stress test, but who puts a 92 year old on a treadmill? He wanted to admit her so that he could monitor her levels through the night. By morning they would have dropped down to normal, and she would be discharged, but my mother, as always, objected strongly to being admitted. I assured her I would check on the cats and close any open windows.

On these overnight hospital stays when I'd stop at my mother's house, I did not like entering her home alone, to try on how it would feel once she was gone. I moved quickly through her rooms, replacing chairs pushed out from her sunroom table, gathering old mugs, teabags dried on their saucers. On her bed, I found the museum catalogue she'd mentioned, open to the puzzle toy, and I was sorry for my quipped remarks in the emergency room —I knew how her days went, lying on her bed, surrounded by those newspapers and catalogues. Time and days now running together, with little to differentiate one hour from the next, except for how the sun set behind the cherry trees outside her windows. Occasionally she'd still draw in a small pocket notebook, and after she died, I'd find sketches of those crooked cherry trees, pen and inks with occasional pastel sweeps to capture the sun's receding brilliance, a new fragility to these landscapes, her dominant hand weakened by arthritis. Her very last sketches would be more scribbles, of the sunflowers she'd ask me to pick up from the market every fall. I would bring her sunflowers weekly in her last year, to stand on the shelf as relief from the medical clutter of bandages for her gangrenous leg. Though by then she would no longer be drawing, would not remember having been an artist at all.

I was fourteen when mother inherited the small weathered Cape-style house from her godmother, perfectly situated one block from the Atlantic Ocean beach in the Hamptons of Long Island, New York. When we drove out there for the first time from where I grew up on Staten Island, we found in the attic old linens and lace, rhinestone-studded Victorian hair combs, boxes of daguerreotypes tucked away under the sweltering eaves. My mother saved these relics, just as she painstakingly preserved much of the old house, stripping the original built-in kitchen hutch down to its natural pine wood, and painting the claw-footed bathtub an aquamarine blue. But as much as the house had its own past, so much of it became imbued with everything about my mother: the bold of modular couches and tribal throw pillows; the massive copper wall sculpture by an artist she admired. Then there were those things too familiar, her St. Francis statue, collection of Raggedy Ann dolls, bowl of beach glass she'd collected over so many years, that after she died, I'd arrange and rearrange to places where they did not so resonate, did not reawaken again in me my longing for her. I'd leaf through the oversized art books I'd never before opened, collected over her entire life time, large old volumes with yellowed tissue protecting the colored El Greco and Picasso prints. I'd weep in her hall closet at the sight of her ceramic plates, much more to her taste than the traditional Dogwood of her wedding china.

After she died, I also would find those things that spoke of my mother in a way I'd never known her, only heard about from the stories she'd tell me. Before my father, she'd had two serious relationships, though both with men she'd been unable to marry; one because she had to be home caring for her parents while her brothers were off in the war; the other, a devout Catholic who could not marry outside of the church, and I'd find an inscription to her, in a Thomas Merton book. Then a pen-and-ink drawing distinctly of my mother, in a bathing suit and sunglasses, and I'd realize one of these men must have been an artist. I'd find her scrapbook from her trip through Italy shortly before she met my father, filled with her sketches, train tickets and Florence postcards.

And then there were those things I'd find that spoke of my mother as I'd never imagined her, as a child. Up in the attic, I'd find memorabilia that evidently made their way back to her once her own parents died—typed letters to her father from Lake Sunapee where she spent her summers while he worked back on Staten Island; an Easter card she drew, of a yellow chick carrying a wagon of eggs up a hill; stories she wrote in large careful cursive, about fairies playing with their dolls as they danced around the moon. I'd find a lock of her hair from when she was a little girl, a brilliant blond so unlike the frosted gray color I'd always known, saved in a tiny envelope labeled "Betty's hair." The house for me would become the wellspring of my mother in all the ways I'd always known her, then in those ways I only would discover after her death.

Before my mother resorted most days to lying on her bed, she loved best sitting on her lounge chair out on the deck where, every morning, she carried a tray with her coffee, a soft-boiled egg, oatmeal with a dollop of blueberry yogurt and sliced banana, and English muffin wrapped in foil. If not the deck, the sunroom where she sat in her favorite Eames-style chair, until she no longer could push herself out of its low-slung seat. My mother always spoke of her home as a "happy house," a place filled with good spirits. But I think for her it was happy because it was the first place she was fully able to come into her own, unlike the house I grew up in on Staten Island. Marrying my father, she was expected to move into another woman's home, my father's first wife having died of cancer. Looking back now, I can see that all those years in the Staten Island house my mother had been honoring my father's first wife's memory for his sake, forsaking her own tastes for the more traditional of Mahogany, of the looming living-room highboy, of drapes and oriental area rugs.

Back on Staten Island, anything that spoke of my mother's life before she married, all her single years living in New York City, seemed relegated to the cellar which was also her studio. I remember her sitting in the shadows, on her couch of a rough woven weave from her apartment in Greenwich Village, with her feet up on her teak coffee table, contemplating a canvas on her easel. My mother painted in that cellar for all of my growing up, her paintings quite literally luminous in an otherwise dark space. We never even referred to that cellar as a basement, too low-ceilinged and with scant natural light. The only truly bright light was a reflective one, off whatever canvas was on her easel, fresh paint glistening in the dull glow of an overhead flood lamp. Everything about that cellar I remember as dark: the black linoleum floor spattered with dried paint; the empty brick fireplace; my mother moving in and out of the shadows to work a painting, her style back then cubist, her inspiration, the sharp angles of the Verrazano bridge viewed from our living-room picture window. She painted mostly in acrylics then, her palette entirely different from her later paintings once my parents moved to Long Island, crimson reds and vibrant greens, and I can wonder now if she wasn't surprised by their color once she took them upstairs into the natural light.

Once I graduated college, my parents moved out to the beach house full-time, adding on a new wing which also included my mother's first real studio. Optimal natural light was paramount, and after she died, I would come across the original blueprints for the studio rolled up in an old filing cabinet—I would think about my mother tweaking the architect's design for the best northern exposure, a more even, uncompromising light, than southern. Two rows of skylights flanked the cathedral ceiling. My mother always had stretched her own canvases, but now she had room to miter them as well, on a large moveable table she had built to fit the space. The scale of her new studio equaled her determination to "make it" as an artist, to take full advantage of a creative space now afforded by this expansive physical one.

In this new space, her cubist style gave way to the more ambient, of the light and expanse of ocean vistas. I was living in New York City by then, going to Columbia University for my MFA in writing, and when I visited, she'd ask me to come in to her studio for my opinion of her latest work. She'd point to where she thought a painting needed a bright spot, scraping the canvas with a finger, her nails always rimmed in blues or yellows—an area she didn't like. "Don't tell me what you think I want to hear," she'd say. "Tell me what you really think." I felt the weight of this, not only in my feeling unqualified to answer, my knowledge of art far more intuitive than learned, all really, and ironically perhaps, what she herself had passed on to me. But she was seeking in her daughter a validation she acutely was missing as an artist, most searingly perhaps, from her own mother who had sent her to Katharine Gibbs to become a secretary. To whom she'd gifted a representational painting of flowers, "Night Garden," her instinct toward the bold and abstract retrained, even in her choice of subject. If I praised her work, my mother would counter with her own self-doubts. Coming from me, it wasn't finally validation, it was just me being a "good daughter."

    I don't remember when exactly my mother stopped painting, when she began to spend more time staring at her canvases than working them, with rags, palette knives and her bare hands, rubbing in sand for texture. My mother's studio was largely the cats' domain now, and I could hear them scurrying behind her painting racks. Tufts of cat fur rolled like tumbleweed across the plywood floor. The old couch was gone, and the teak coffee table she'd passed on to me for my own apartment. The original tin table from the kitchen housed her coffee cans of paintbrushes stiff and dried. Empty stretchers were stacked against the wall. On her work table was a plastic crate of dried seaweed, driftwood and other beach finds she'd saved over years, always imagining using them in collage. After she died, I would find her first oil set from when she was ten, a rusted tin with the original paints, some miraculously still solvent. Though I'd never seen it before, she'd mentioned the tin over the years, in stories she told about painting out in her rowboat those summers on Lake Sunapee.

    On her easel now was her last painting, a kind of white moon scrubbed across an unfinished canvas, but I don't imagine there came a day when she decided never to paint again. Rather, it seemed a gradual relinquishing after my father died, when she would complain about how hard it was to "get back into it after being away," although she hadn't been anywhere. I think it was less about being away than it was about the fact that it was the first time she did not have someone to take care of; she was not used to claiming her time as her own. My father spent his last two years in a nursing home, and my mother spent those years fretting about the fact that she had placed him in a home. Before that, there were the many years she'd watched his mind gradually dwindle. Once they'd moved to Long Island, he would get lost walking up to the post office, and the police would find him wandering in a neighboring potato field. Sometimes he would rise suddenly from a chair, thinking he had to be somewhere, to catch some train. He once found the car keys and drove off, having forgotten he hadn't driven in over twenty years. The police found him wandering the streets the next town over, having forgotten where he'd parked the car. My father was twenty years older than my mother, and over the course of thirteen years, gradually the present seemed to recede into the past, and then the more distant past, when every night he would ask whether his brother, a bombing pilot whose plane was blown out of the sky in World War I, was joining us for dinner.

My mother finally placed him in a nursing home when he lost all sense of real time, up most nights getting dressed to make his own breakfast at 2 am and leaving oatmeal to burn on the stove. Even though he was only in the nursing home for a couple of years, placing him in one my mother would always regret. She would rake back over what she could have or should have done, as thoroughly as she used to turn over the earth every spring in her vegetable garden—and like the garden which somehow only produced sporadic misshapen squash, the raking proved futile. What my mother forgot in her circling guilt, was she'd taken care of my father for as long as she could manage, her only reprieve, the two days a week when she put him on a minibus to the adult day-care center. She would be waiting at the door when he returned, to exude over his child-like drawings of misshapen Santas and little clay figurines as she only ever had with me.

That my mother would be allowed to die in her "happy" house was an unspoken promise between us. I say unspoken, because I could no more imagine my mother in a nursing facility than I could myself. Despite my promise, rooted in her was a real fear that her independence would be seized, snatched as suddenly as things could seem to happen, whether by another fall, a dropped plate she no longer could balance, or just a leaking pipe. Her own mother and godmother both wound up in nursing homes, and I remember visiting my grandmother—playing jacks in the courtyard directly beneath her window so that I could see her there, ghostly but peaceful somehow, against the reflection of the maple trees. "Your grandmother had the temperament," my mother would say; she may not have been happy in the nursing home, but she was no more *un*happy than her usual depressive disposition. My mother's godmother, Aunt Didi, on the other hand, had lived a vibrant life—a vibrancy instantly drained from her when it was my mother's brother who placed her in a nursing home. My mother would tell me about visiting her and finding Aunt Didi "slumped" in a chair. It was my mother who took her out of the nursing home, moved her into an apartment, and for those last years, managed the care of in-home aides, now for her godmother as well as her mother. Because that would be my mother too, she claimed. She too would slump in a chair.

What I hadn't foreseen was that her "happy" house would become between us a bone—a structure—of contention, as we both vied for its control. It would become one of pure portent; I could not see past the chaos of newspapers and catalogues, to the beautiful old chests that had been there forever, what I would not take real notice of until she was gone. The small things now became crises, the wall switch to the overhead kitchen light that failed, the washing machine that broke, the black smoke spewing from the basement because it had been so long since she'd had the oil burner cleaned. She would hire more than one landscaper, not remembering having contracted with another, and both would show up with their big mowers.

When I discovered a pipe leaking in the basement, she did not have a plumber.

"I don't remember ever having a plumber," she said. Of course, by then she couldn't remember a lot of things.

I'd gone down to the basement because the hot water to the claw-footed tub in the guest bathroom wasn't working —a tub rarely used, except my mother had finally relented to having an aide come for the week while she was recovering from rib contusions after falling into the corner of the television.

Descending into that deep dank dark was like climbing down into the actual earth, part of the floor still sand. Peeling a spider-web-mask off my face so I could actually look up at the pipes, I located the hot water valve— evidently, someone, some time long ago, when that guest bath was still in use, had turned it off.

And with good reason—I turned it on, and hot water spurted from the pipes.

"Get my address book," she said. "If you can find it, I swear, there's a gremlin in the house..."

I'd settled her into her lounge chair out on the deck, with bed pillows supporting her sides.

I found her address book where I expected to find it, under a pile of newspapers. And tucked into the pages, a pile of unpaid bills—dating back at least a couple of months. I felt heat rise up into my face. My hands went numb.

"Oh, you found it!" she exclaimed, when I came back out to the deck. "Where was it?"

I shook the bills at her. "What *is* all this?"

"Who said you could go through my things?"

I stood there, clamping and unclamping my fists, crumpling the bills.

"I put them there so I'd remember to pay them."

"And then you lost your *address* book."

"I didn't lose it...I knew it would show up sooner or later."

This reasoning was as reasonable as Owen claiming he only "forgot" leaving a jar of worms to roast on the swing because he "didn't remember."

"*Mom.*"

"Oh, Sandy, don't start," she said, her voice quivering in that way that only riled me.

"You're lucky your water hasn't been turned off!" I'd been wanting to take over her bills for some time, and she had been insistent that she could handle it. I felt triumphant.

My mother looked stonily out at her bird feeder. "Go get me the phone book."

A phone book? Really? The thing I was learning on this new learning curve of daughter-having-to-take-care-of-mother, is that the issue of control was a delicate one. I grit my teeth. Ground them, to keep myself from spewing profanities.

I got the phone book. Dutifully, I handed it to her.

She started perusing the plumbing section as if it were just another catalogue.

My jaw ached.

She began reading out loud that very, very fine disclaimer print no one ever reads: the phone book folk "can't guarantee" that the plumbing folk "adhere to licensing requirements" etc. Like the fine print on those book-length medical printouts that come with every tiny bottle of medication, about all the side effects, which if you were to actually read, you would never take the medication in the first place. As she could indeed, refuse to take her pills.

As I listened to her reciting the phone book, I saw a deer in her woods, behind her forsythia bush. Where my mother lived, deer were so prevalent, most people put up mesh fences around their gardens, and sprayed their front-stoop seasonal petunias and mums with deer repellant. My mother didn't spray nor put up fences, though she could complain about the deer eating away all the lower branches of her evergreens and snowball bushes. She rarely shooed them away, knowing they had come up this far from the dunes because they were hungry. And if I was there, we would both grow as still and silent as we had all those years ago, up at that Vermont lake, when spotting deer was truly a thrill, as they rarely emerged in broad daylight. Nights driving back from dinner in town, our headlights might wash over one so that their eyes glowed, suspended in the dark like small moons. "Oh, *look*," my mother would exhale, in a reverent hush, as she still could some forty years later when one showed up, like this, on the edge of her woods.

I knew she never got tired of seeing them, that bit of wildness at the edge of her garden. She would have enjoyed the distraction now.

I didn't draw her attention to the deer. She needed a plumber and, instead, was reading the phone book to me. I snatched it away.

"Oh, don't be so *impatient*!"

"You think I want this, to be dealing with leaking pipes right now?" I said, with a sweeping gesture at her awkward posture, propped up on those pillows that had to be rearranged every half hour because her ribs would begin to hurt.

"I will get a plumber," she said evenly.

"You won't."

"You of little faith. You forget, I've been taking care of myself since I was eighteen."

Which lead her to reciting that old story again, about

how she had taken care of both her parents, since her father lost everything in the Great Depression, then had a stroke, again, how she supported them on half her salary. This was a story I'd been hearing all of my life, and at various times, it resonated deeply for me; my mother had always been the epitome of strength and endurance. But as she repeated this story in those last years, in my own panic and frustration, I might counter with the fact that she no longer *was* eighteen.

As I did now. As I yelled, loud enough to frighten the deer: "You're not *eighteen* anymore!"

With a great rustle, the deer sprang back into my mother's overgrown brushes.

My mother shook her finger at me. Shaking the very foundation of her lounge chair: "Don't you dare put me in a *home*!"

What she expected of me perhaps, was to assure her once again, that I would never put her in a home. I didn't. I could hear my heart pounding in my chest in the silence that followed. Because in that moment, her threats only emboldened me to rebel, as much as I would be ashamed, even mortified, by my inability to rise above my own childish petulance.

I said nothing. I got up to go inside to call a plumber from the phone book. Though I could still see her. How I'd left her alone out on the deck, my own chair pushed out at a sharp angle. Because I could imagine how that moment should have been: our watching the deer together, as it turned and bounded back into the trees, the white of its tail a flash of welcomed light.

4

Up until the last call my mother made to me, on the day she was dying, barely a day went by when we didn't talk on the phone. And after we'd hang up, one or the other would call back about something we'd forgotten—my mother to remind me to pick up a box of kitty litter, too heavy for her to carry home herself, or me to remind her of the breaded cutlets I'd made for her, in the freezer. As time went on, our conversations would become primarily about her own crises: the "gremlin" in the house who took not only her glasses and her address book, but her pill bottles, misplaced checkbooks or car keys. She'd call me in a panic, thinking her purse was stolen, until it was returned from the IGA where she'd left it in her shopping cart. But she also could call just because, flipping through another catalogue, she'd come across something else she thought would make a good present for the boys. Or just because she had to tell me about the "whole bevy" of wild turkeys who appeared "out of nowhere" in her backyard.

When the boys were toddlers, I called her most days around lunch time, once I'd put them down for their nap, and my mother was eating a bowl of barley or lentil soup. If she was having her soup in the sunroom, she'd tell me about the young doe that came to drink from her birdbath. I would think out loud to her about how I'd noticed my first real wrinkle.

My then 93-year-old mother chuckled. "Your *first*?"

"It's not even a laugh line." I was upset. "This is my first *real* wrinkle. It's there all the time."

"Try hemorrhoid cream, like Doreen does." Doreen, at the time was the one who came to help my mother, one of the many well-intended but inept souls who came and went.

"On your *face*?"

"She has flawless skin and is about your age."

This wasn't what I was looking for. "I'm not putting something on my face that goes on your butt."

"Well, then you have to start using serum and a good brand of wrinkle cream."

"I use moisturizer."

"That's not wrinkle cream."

True. I'd avoided anything labelled for wrinkles. Yes, I had some laugh lines and a few crow's feet, but not *wrinkles*.

She laughed. "Wait until you get a turkey neck."

Before I had children and was trying to get pregnant, there were those phone calls when I just needed to hear the sound of my mother's voice. After I found out I had miscarried, I called her from the beach where I'd parked my car. The doctor had pointed to the hazy bean-shaped image on the screen, to where the heart should have been beating. I'd called Derek at work, and could feel him, for my sake, trying to rise up out of his own well of disappointment—I told him he did not need to come home, that I would be all right. Which I thought I would be, until I was driving home and could not fathom walking into the empty house, to where I'd left my coffee on the counter, the mug still half full—from the time before, when it had not occurred to me that our baby's heart could have stopped beating without my ever having known.

On my flip phone, I'd sobbed openly to my mother and she said, "Oh honey, I hate to see you like this..." There was nothing she could say to make me feel better, but she was able to share in my pain; I knew she was more upset by my devastation than by the loss of our baby, and therein lay the comfort. One I don't think Derek and I could have afforded each other, not until later, after we'd had the time to digest the news separately. When finally I was pregnant with Lucas, I called her after the sonogram; I'd found out I was having a boy, and I only knew about mothers and daughters. "What am I going to do with a *boy*?" I cried, until we were both laughing.

After Lucas, I would have Owen just seventeen months later, and so it was the boys I often talked about, relating their latest antics of running outside in their diapers to watch the garbage trucks or taking down all my books to play "library," and my mother would laugh and tell me I should be writing all this down. This only irritated me—I seemed to have lost all capacity for written words, never mind cohesive thoughts. I'd wanted this, to be a stay-at-home mom. I didn't want to miss their sucking on popsicles to melt down their arms, climbing into laundry baskets to scoot across the floor. But I also missed the immersive of writing, of *being* a writer, never more content than when I was working on a novel. Rather, I'd always been the least restive. Because even in those spaces in between, when I wasn't writing, I would be thinking about it, the next chapter, the scene that needed revising. Unlike in the spaces I had now, when it was the boys who were most content, engrossed as they plowed their tractors through the sandbox, while I seemed reduced to a kind of stupor.

This perhaps is the dichotomy of motherhood: at once too much space and not enough. But these alone times with my toddlers I found easier than the "playdates," enforced socialization as much for us moms as for our children; us stay-at-home moms were schooled together in a way we never would have been otherwise, around the library train table on our knees, helping our toddlers push the wooden trains around the tracks, or at Gymboree, billowing one large communal parachute over our children's heads. I hadn't been prepared for this facelessness of motherhood, how we seemed only able to talk about our children without ever talking about ourselves. I would know some of these women for years, running into them at pick-up when our kids came streaming out of the elementary school, without them ever knowing I was a writer. I would only find out one was a dental hygienist when she would go back to work for my dentist and clean my teeth.

When I joined the Mother's Center, a dank place in the basement of the Presbyterian church, where mothers congregated with their strollers to find a comradery, I'd tell my mother about meetings I'd attend, where we swapped birthing stories and our views on the controversy of vaccines, and how I found myself struggling to fit in as I hadn't struggled since Junior High—back when sameness mattered more than differentiation, when I was hiding who I really was, now, a frustrated writer. How I was thinking of quitting the center, preferring my own company, and my mother would say, "Oh, Sandy, don't be like me."

She could go on then about regretting turning down lunch invites because it interrupted her time in the studio, regretting since moving to Long Island not having fostered closer friendships for the support she now wished for in her old age, for not "making the effort to be more social." At the same time, my mother recognized my discontent for what it was; for the first time in my life, I had no creative outlet independent of my children. I was feeling failed as a writer, and falsely believed having babies could make up for that failure; that I could *write* my children, in a way they quickly proved to be writing themselves. And so my mother could also say, "you have to find your happiness from within."

But these conversations could sometimes lead elsewhere, back to herself and her own feelings of failure. "How do you think *I* feel?" she'd interject. "At the end of my life now and having nothing to show for it." This was something in our phone calls over those last years she would voice again and again, when she no longer was painting, her last attempts at small pastels or sketches only exacerbating her frustration. I knew she was talking about believing she had not reached her full potential as an artist, and I found those calls especially hard.

Still. I could take an only-child childish offense and quip, "Well, you had *me*..." resisting reminding her of calling me Rosebud in the hospital; of how I had been her "miracle", after trying for five years for a baby; of what she'd always told me, her astonishment and pure delight when the rabbit test was positive, of what I assumed: having a baby would have fulfilled her in a way that being an artist never could.

Her silence on the line could reverberate across the distance between us, our two points on the map, on the different stages of our lives. Then she would only say, "Well, of *course*, but..." She never finished the sentence, as how could she? How could she explain that, referentially, as to her life as an artist, not as a mother, I was entirely beside the point?

She didn't need to explain. Because I was already learning about the referential part; the uncomfortable truth about motherhood, that we cannot finally sustain ourselves so selflessly—not even my mother could, despite my having been her miracle. And I can wonder whether as the days drew on, with nursing and sleeplessness, with the mindless monotony of giving, whether she too must have begun to miss that space she could call her own.

The only time we went without talking on the phone, was when she left her phone off the hook. Rather, she'd neglect to hit the "Off" button on her cordless which increasingly she would mistake for TV remote control. Sometimes it would be a full day before I could get through, and energized by pure worry, I took to vacuuming up Goldfish from between all the seat cushions, scrubbing mildew from around the shower tiles, wondering whether I should call the police, whether she'd slipped in the shower and cracked her skull on the edge of the tub.

Eventually she'd be the one to call me and snipe, "Oh. Well, I thought you'd dropped off the face of the earth."

In my daughterly defense, I let her know I had a Verizon customer service rep check her line, to confirm that the busy signal meant that her phone was off the hook. This most frequently was the case when she'd "hang up" the phone by merely placing it face down on her comforter. "It wasn't off the hook," she'd claim—quite definitively. "It's broken. I need new phones."

The needing of new phones was an argument I most often lost. We could spend an entire phone call arguing about phones: "Why don't you ever believe me," she'd fret, interrupting whatever I was saying to complain about our connection. Complaints about my voice fading in and out or the static *she* could hear at *her* end, and to appease her, I'd go out and buy a whole new set at Best Buy. I shouldn't have been surprised to find after she died, a basket full of tangled discarded—and no doubt—perfectly good phones.

So seamlessly were these phone conversations sewn into the fabric of my days, that when she called those times when I had just been out to see her, it was as if I hadn't left. Except I had and would not be able to help her with things like her remote control when she couldn't get the TV to go on. In winter, I often was driving home at dusk, into a setting sun, whose crimson and lavender hues reminded me of her paintings. I could hear my mother exclaiming, "Oh, just *look* at that *sky*!" and I would be missing her, as I could, as if she were already gone. Until I walked in the door, and the phone rang.

And it was my *mother*.

"I can't get it open. The chicken."

I hadn't had time to freeze some meals for her, so I'd bought her a rotisserie chicken. Often resorting to these precooked chickens for ourselves, I was familiar with the "convenience" of this container, a plastic lid fitted over a black plastic base.

Well, I'd *assumed* it was convenient....

"It has a lid on it," I said. "Take the lid off."

"I'm not an imbecile, I know it's got a lid. I haven't *completely* lost it..." she snipped, the kind of comment she'd make when I reminded her about an upcoming doctor's appointment; one she might remember was on a Friday, but unable to find her datebook, neglects to write down which Friday.

There was a loud raucous crackling of plastic. "I've been struggling with this for *hours*..."

If I hadn't just seen her, it *could* actually have been hours. As long as she could pour over those charitable solicitations, catalogues, or the fine print of phone books.

"The lid has a little lip or handle on one corner," I said. "Lift that up."

"There's no lip. It's sealed shut."

I knew this was going to be a long call, and wished I'd let the answering machine pick her up, although she would have just rattled on, anyway. I put my own phone on speaker like she hated, so that I could put her on the counter. Our own dinner was burning—too late. The rice was stuck to the bottom of the pot. The broccoli reduced to mush. Just how the boys refused to eat it, "puke green and mushy." It was hard enough to produce for them the perfect palatable texture without simultaneously helping my mother to open a plastic chicken container long distance.

With the speaker on, the plastic crackling grew louder, like a super bad phone connection.

Owen suddenly appeared in front of me—as he could, honestly, like magic: "Mom, I have a new trick to show you."

Owen laid out pompom balls on the kitchen counter to make them disappear beneath plastic cups. As he would make a nickel disappear. He liked to make things disappear.

"That's so magical, incredible," I effused, to make up for the incredible fact that I wasn't really watching. Which he realized, anyhow, and didn't care; he could practice just as well in front of the dog.

"Who's that?" came my mother's voice far too succinctly from the counter.

"Me, Gramma," Owen said.

The crackling grew louder—no reception issues on *our* end.

"I'm taking a steak knife to it," Gramma said.

Owen's eyes widened. "A knife? To what?"

"A chicken," I said, distractedly, cursing internally, somewhere deep down in my bowels—I'd neglected to put our own main course in the oven. Chicken. Drumsticks.

My six year old's big blue eyes grew bigger. "Gramma's killing a chicken?"

"Damn it. This is so *stupid!*" came Gramma's too-loud voice.

We both looked at her; a cordless phone.

Owen's surprised look turned to scorn. "Why's it always ok for Gramma to say 'damn it' and not us?"

The crackling stopped for a moment. "Owen, is that you? Damn is not a good word, you're right…"

"Gramma, what are you doing to a chicken?"

Then came my mother's voice small and tinny behind

the loud crackling of plastic. "Just trying to open it, Dear."

Then Lucas came in with finger extended: "Mom, I need a Band-Aid."

He held out his pinky.

"Not this minute."

"It *hurts*. I can't do anything. I can't even practice my guitar."

Now I was feeling harassed. I picked back up the phone, and turning away from them, whispered in my most pacifying voice, one that I tried to hold just steady enough so that I could sound more daughterly than patronizing: "Mom, I don't think it's actually sealed shut."

"Of *course* it is. Then why otherwise would it take me hours to open a container of chicken?" I could hear her stabbing at it now, at the plastic container. "Oh, *why* does everything have to be so complicated?"

There was truth to this. As much as she would argue with me about the phones, I could see how it could seem reasonable enough just to put the receiver back in the cradle like the old rotary phones of my childhood, than to have to press an "Off" button.

"I can't even open a simple bottle of seltzer anymore." She sounded close to tears. Her arthritis in her right hand was especially bothersome, probably from so many years of wielding painting brushes, clamping a staple gun when stretching her canvases.

"Mom, we should get someone to look at that hand."

She didn't seem to hear me, fixated on her frustration at the moment.

"Oh, how I *hate* growing old. Don't. Grow. *Old!*"

I tried to walk her through dissecting the chicken container. "Slip the knife in between the clear plastic top section and bottom section."

"Don't you think I tried that? Just horrendous that anyone would do this to a person," she complained as she would about the childproof pill bottles not even an adult could open. "This is not good for my blood pressure!"

"What's Gramma *doing*?" Lucas asked, forgetting all about his finger.

"Gramma's killing a chicken." Owen now was dreamily just spinning the little balls around on the counter. "She's opening it up."

"Wait, I'm getting it," my mother said. "I'm just going to...hold on. I need two hands."

She was the one to put me on speaker now, dropping the phone no doubt, onto the butcher's block table so it sounded like she'd dropped it down a bone-dry well.

"There. I *got* it."

There was a moment of quiet, a calm at both ends of our landlines.

She would again forget to press the "Off" button, and I would listen as she rustled around the kitchen, talking to herself as she could, about why did everything have to be so "complicated." But it was one more small crisis averted, and the boys were relieved that the chicken she was "killing" was already dead.

5

Besides talking on the phone, there were other constants in our relationship, times framed primarily within the years after my father died and before I married. By that time, I was living and working in New York City, and weekends, I often took the Long Island Railroad to East Hampton. My mother picked me up in whatever van she had at the time, the boxy dinged up one she bought second-hand, before her last van, the blue Ford. She'd always driven a van so that she could transport her large paintings to and from exhibitions.

If it was summer, we went to the bay most afternoons, swimming laps between the rocky peninsulas of the Devon and Little Albert Landing beaches. We sat in our folding chairs, my mother wearing one of my father's Oxford shirts to shield herself from the sun, with a straw sunhat arched over her face. She always brought a sketchbook and a couple of black felt-tip pens in a reusable cloth tote from the local library, and make quick sketches of people on the beach—she'd laugh in frustration when someone would move and she'd lose their pose. I'd bring a book, though I rarely got much reading done, both of us distracted by terns dive-bombing; seagulls scavenging for crabs and potato chips; toddlers whom my mother especially rejoiced in watching, collecting pebbles along the rocky shore. If it was a Sunday, there was the sailing race next door at the yacht club. White sails billowed like clouds in late afternoon light winds.

We stayed at the beach until it got cool or the flies got to be too much, however much we tried to cover our legs with our towels. Saturday evenings, there were art openings at the local galleries, and we'd go home to shower and change—I would always be ready before my mother, as she would spread out different amalgams of outfits on her bed, unable to decide what to wear. She would change from her daily shoulder leather bag, to her smaller handwoven one with the ceramic button. Sometimes it was my mother's own art openings, once at the Benton Gallery in Bridgehampton, where I met one of my boyfriends—for three years, I was going out there more frequently, until we broke up because he didn't want to marry and have children.

Once a summer she usually held a party for the local artists' alliance out on her deck, and I'd help to serve drinks and her appetizers carefully arranged on her various wood platters from New England gift shops. Those were the years when finally, she was able to come into her own in the art community, to establish connections that she hadn't so easily been able to when taking care of my father —this hiatus, a first in her entire life, from caregiving, until she herself required care.

And invariably, whenever I visited, we went out to dinner. When my father was alive, we had a favorite restaurant where he'd order their chocolate truffle cake for dessert. We went there so frequently as a family, that the owners knew us by name and would serve the chocolate cake on the house whenever it was my father's birthday. The first time I remember my mother and I going there just the two of us, was a gray night in March after visiting my father in the nursing home. That night was clearly a marker for me; unlike our usual table in a corner for three, we sat at a small table for only two, between the front windows. Through the sheer café curtains, I could see the window boxes that had been cleared of Christmas greens, but it was too early yet for spring pansies—they were dark and blank. We had just driven the hour drive back from the nursing home in Riverhead where we had seen my father for the last time before he died.

It was around St. Patrick's day, because at the nursing home, there was a construction-paper cutout of a green clover taped to my father's door. A doctor had called my mother that morning to tell her that my father had gone into heart failure, having turned blue while eating breakfast. I met my mother at the nursing home in Riverhead, taking a cab from the train station. My mother was sitting with my father whose bed had been wheeled out into the hall because they were waxing the floors. She was upset about his being stuck in the hall, and distracted herself by looking at the newspaper—which struck me at the time as unbelievable: *how could she read the paper when Daddy was dying?* Years later, when it was me being summoned to my mother's side, I would better understand how checking the latest headlines in the world beyond this awful insular one, was a coming up for air, from the dank and lonely depths of the present crisis.

My father kept reaching for the railings, trying to pull himself up, scissoring his legs, a look of utter terror on his face—he too must have known that he was dying. Though at the time, I could only see the terror. I leaned down into his face to whisper whatever I could think of, to purely soothe, as years later I would with my children waking from nightmares, or with Lucas before his surgery when he dislocated is hip. I rambled on about the first thing that came into my head, and that was about our summers at the Vermont lake. I told him we would motor over to Bird's store. After a swim, we would get used to the water by standing in the shallows together, before he dove in the way I remember, at once forceful and with tremendous grace. We would feed the fish off the dock as we sometimes did, scraps from our dinner plates, and laugh at the sunfish fighting over strands of spaghetti.

By late afternoon, the floors were dried, and he was wheeled back into his room. We stayed until dark, and by the time we left, I could see egg from his breakfast still caught in his gold fillings, his mouth gaping open as he faded in and out of consciousness. We stayed until we were both depleted. I drove us back to Amagansett, my mother too tired to drive. "I won't be able to cope," she'd said, when we debated staying the night. I realize now she was probably worried about coping with the logistics of death, logistics she already knew well from her godmother and own mother, as well as of one of her other brothers who had died of stomach cancer. Logistics I would only truly come to know when it was my turn to be executor, for my mother's estate.

We ordered Dewar's on the rocks, and the truffle dessert to share in honor of "Daddy." My mother was somewhere between tearful and faint, just moving her fork around the plate, not really eating. I think she understood what I didn't, that Daddy would die before dawn. My mother had hired a full-time nurse for overnight, and the nurse called at 3:30 am to tell us he had just died—"passed so peacefully," at first she though he was only sleeping. Just before the phone call, my mother and I both had woken up, unable to go back to sleep. To this day, I'm sure it was my father nudging us both gently, tapping into us just insistently enough to say goodbye, as surprised as we were that he was actually gone.

After my father died, I came out weekends more often, as much for me as for my mother. Losing my father was my first real loss and I needed my mother to help me navigate it, though, ultimately, we navigated it as different continents, each with its own rough terrains. While I cannot remember our actual conversations, I remember how those dinners went, my mother holding the candle to a menu so that she could see better, our sharing a plate of mussels. She often wore her big brass starburst pendant, her favorite bracelets of soldered nails, and one of her colorful scarves to hide her "turkey neck." There was always about her the fragrance of face powder, as she never went out without first putting on "a new face." I remember how she ate: one hand resting on the table with a thumb pointed out. She'd cuss if she spilled on her blouse and dip her napkin in her water glass. Wherever we went, she would order either salmon or chicken as she was forever trying to lower her triglycerides; occasionally a steak with a salad; on special days, we'd share a dessert. Sometimes chocolate cake again.

What I can't remember is what exactly we talked about. Maybe because I can imagine it was mostly me doing the talking, rambling on about whatever was going on in my life, thinking out loud as I could to her; part of me still the little girl who could sit on her mother's lap and tell her endless stories, real and imagined, one idea blooming into another, without a hint of self-consciousness. What I do remember are her responses. Her exuberance, sometimes even with a little clap her hands, "This is *such* fun!" And "Oh it's so good to see you so happy!" Or: "Oh, honey I hate to see you this way..." Her iron staples of love.

All those years of our traditional dinners out, I never thought there would actually be a very last time we would go out to a restaurant. It was soon after a full-time aide moved into her "happy" house, and we went to another favorite restaurant, one in the Springs, where we always requested a booth with the soft cushions. This time we had to sit at a table, on hard chairs. My mother's hard chair was so uncomfortable she had to fold up her coat to sit on it, but it kept slipping off the chair—I did not have her usual undivided attention, as she was continuously shifting the coat, unable to get comfortable. And dressing to go out: it had been an ordeal, her near tears trying to figure out what to wear, as she emptied her closet. "You're rattling me, *both* of you go away!" she yelled, resisting either me or her aide helping to pull up her good black pants.

She hadn't bothered with her pendant and bracelets, only a scarf that was half hanging off her neck. Even though the restaurant was stifling, she complained she was cold. Clearly, this was a *huge* mistake, but she still made the effort to be there for me in that way she always had been, when she wasn't twisting uncomfortably in her chair, and running her hands up and down her arms to get warm. Looking back, I can wonder, whose idea *was* this? Probably both of ours, as we were desperately seeking some kind of the old normality. And we both wanted to escape this stranger living under her roof. We didn't order dessert, nor finish our entrees, having them packed up to bring home as leftovers. I think she even cut me off mid-sentence: "I need to go home."

The other constant: summer trips to New England. Except for when she took me to New Mexico and Florence, we always drove up north, seeking open fields, dilapidated barns, lakes. We sought out the familiar of Route 91, driving up through Connecticut, Massachusetts, sometimes as far as New Hampshire or Vermont. "It's just *gorgeous*!" my mother would exclaim, as the highway, flanked by fields of wild daisies and black-eyed Susans, wound up into the Appalachian mountains, their peaks shifting shades of lavender beneath passing clouds. Like our dinners out, I can't remember these actual trips, beyond the sensory: the sound of crickets at night, of cicadas in long grasses, lightning bugs against our screen windows; the scent of sap and pine walking along wooded paths; the quaint of inns with their country curtains hemmed with hearts; the quiet reverence of meandering gift shops brimming with the handcrafted, wood bowls and pottery, handblown-glass goblets, with the unique: "Look, Sandy...how *cunning*," my mother might say about some hand-sewn cat door stopper. One summer, I bought a hand-painted wall clock and she a quilt that I still keep on her couch in the living room. On her kitchen chimney hang an assortment brass bed warmers and pie tins she picked up at antique stores. I once found an old copper boiler where I still keep my firewood.

I've always been sketching, but never regularly, except on these trips with my mother. "You could have been an artist if you wanted" she'd say, sometimes lamenting about how she thought I drew better than she did, that I didn't get so "noodled." I didn't think about whether I was any good or not—I didn't take drawing seriously in the way she did as an artist. For me, it was all about being in the moment, wherever we were, settled into our folding chairs, on the side of some dirt road or in a field of wild flowers, most often wherever there was a dilapidated old barn to draw. I might remember these places if I come across an old sketch, like one of a couple of abandoned barns in Ludlow, Vermont, a pen-and-ink with washes of watercolor. I remember sitting in that field, looking over at my mother through tall grasses, settled into her own chair, drawing the same barns but from her own carefully chosen perspective.

I can't remember all the places we stayed, but like those dinners, I can remember the very last place: I was six months pregnant. Derek had to work, so it was just me and my mother. The cottage was off a dirt road behind a farmhouse, with its own little overgrown yard. There were a couple of plastic Adirondack chairs, and a rotting picnic table, where the owner had left us a sad little jelly jar of wilting wild flowers. I don't know how we found that place, any of the places we stayed, as it wasn't like we could just go online. But somehow all the places we stayed were either a real hit or a real miss—hit were the charming, rustic and clean. The miss was the moldy, or at Bed and Breakfasts, too-talkative hosts before we'd even had our coffee. And *this* place.

Inside this god-awful little bungalow, it was cool and shadowy, and our bedrooms felt close, with low ceilings and the beds too big for the spaces. There must have been a window in the living room, though I only remember old paneling painted white, and a sunken red couch along one wall. The kitchen seemed an afterthought—attached like some shed, down a couple of stone steps.

The bugs: we didn't notice them at first, so tiny and white, they blended into the scratchy sheets. What we first noticed were the mouse droppings in the kitchen, under the stove burners when we were boiling water in a rusted kettle, then in the drawer—we washed all the silverware. We didn't immediately complain, as my mother had mice at home in her kitchen, and yes, the occasional mouse dropping in a drawer. Mostly, her mice kept to themselves, under the refrigerator evidently, as the cats would lie in wait for them. My mother could feel sorry for them as she did the deer, so she never set traps.

So at least for the first day, we made the best of it. There was morning sun in the little yard, and we had our coffee sitting in the plastic chairs. In the afternoon, we went into whatever town there was, seeking out the gift shops, and my mother bought a teething blanket of a little lamb for the baby. We found a small lake and sat in our folding chairs at the beach—I belabored a lopsided blanket I was crocheting, thinking baby, not sketching. I would feel him kick and withdraw into that private moment alone, wish myself anywhere by here.

I had been itching on and off, but it was the one morning when I woke up with little red welts. I crouched at eye level with the bed—the sun beamed through the one small window, oval like porthole in the bowels of a ship. The minuscule multi-legged little horrors were as perfectly spotlit as if on their own stage. I yelled for my mother who appeared in her satin nightgown, ghostly in the shadowy doorway. No, she hadn't noticed "any bugs," but neither had she the mosquitoes the night before, when we'd tried to eat dinner out at the picnic table. They swarmed to me instead. "My skin is just too old and leathery for their taste," she'd said, contentedly sipping a glass of wine.

This infuriated me, that she didn't have a single red blotch on her. "We're leaving," I said, throwing my clothes into my suitcase, when I should have thrown everything in plastic bags to wash at home; I would have the car sanitized.

My mother did not challenge me. She began packing herself, though tearfully. "Oh, Sandy, I'm so sorry. We shouldn't have come."

And I knew *she* knew my irritableness was not finally about the bugs, not about this disaster of a rental. It was my mother realizing her biggest fear: that she was already becoming a burden. The fact was, I hadn't wanted to come on this trip. I wanted to be back home in my own house, where my heart now resided. With my new husband and a nursery that still needed painting. But neither had I known how to say no when my mother suggested we go up to New England, trips she still looked forward to because she no longer had that, a future she could build for herself. She had only whatever time was left to her, to "try and make it" as an artist, though she already was spending less and less time in her studio. "I don't want you to ever feel I'm a burden," she had said to me over and over through the years after my father died. "You're not a burden," I would always tell her—truthfully, she had never felt like one. Not until this resentment manifesting itself as irritation because of bedbugs. What was finally a harbinger of all that was still to come.

6

There was a trajectory to these final years, and I'm reminded of the winding dirt road along the Rio Chama River, where my mother took me in New Mexico, a place she returned to several times in her youth, to ride horseback through the painted desert of red rock. I would find one black-and-white photo of her leaning on a horse ring. She's in a white blouse, her wavy hair blowing in the dry wind. She is relaxed and happy, clearly in her element. She would tell me about riding a horse down a mountain in a lightning storm, and how "crazy" but exhilarating it was. I often have imagined her in that same blouse, her hair in the wind, riding down that mountain. I imagine her exposed to wind and sky, riding through sage brush and cotton woods, her white blouse brilliant against deepening clouds.

She took me to New Mexico after my father died, and this winding dirt road was off the main paved one to Ghost Ranch, the home of Georgia O'Keefe, located in the "thin space," between the corporal and spiritual, framed by 700-ft cliff faces of Mesozoic sedimentary rock. As we were leaving the ranch, we saw a sign for a monastery "just 13 miles" off the main road, and we made the detour. What we didn't account for was how long a distance 13 miles is when you can only drive five-miles an hour on, not only a winding, but steep and most rocky, dirt road. It was already late afternoon, the shadows deepening across the mountains—our curiosity was met with some trepidation. But there was quite literally no turning back, no room to safely turn around on the one-lane road without rolling into a ditch on one side, off the edge of a steep incline on the other. We continued on, surprised again and again by sharp veers along the edge of the valley. But even if we could have turned around earlier, we probably wouldn't have. This moment held us captive: the receding sun transforming the layered quartz and siltstone, hills of disintegrating gypsum and sandstone. I can hear my mother: "Oh, it's *gorgeous*!"

It was dusk when we finally were able to turn around, in a park overlook, but not without first walking down to the river, where we looked back up at the cascading cliffs; this is what I would miss most, our seizing of the moment. But at this juncture in our trajectory, seizing a moment took on a whole new meaning. There was not time for vistas. Because from the time I dropped off the boys at school to drive to my mother's, then to drive back to pick them up, I was rushing. Time was stretched taut between our two points on the map—the two places I needed to be.

Time, quite literally, was of real essence, especially if we had errands, and to keep my mother from driving, I volunteered that I "enjoyed" accompanying her, whether to CVS, for a haircut, two towns over to K-mart, or for doctor appointments. Which I did not *enjoy*—expeditions really, that only stretched time more taut, to a real breaking point. But neither did I want to risk her venturing out in her van—dinged-up from various minor scrapes—beyond the one-block radius of the post office and grocery store, as increasingly, I worried about her reaction time behind the wheel. So I would switch her handicapped tag to my own minivan, as I did not trust that her old van wouldn't break down; neither of us could remember the last time she'd had the oil changed.

All facets of these expeditions had to be accounted for: the time it took my mother to navigate down the front steps, to the gravel driveway, to the car; to settle into the front seat so that I could finagle her seatbelt over her bulky coat she wore even in warm weather because she was always cold; at the IGA, the time it took her to pick out cat food—I would speed-walk up and down the aisles, collecting her staples of orange juice, English muffins, eggs, eye-of-the-round steaks, spaghetti and low-salt Nabisco crackers, to find her still deliberating between Purina or Fancy Feast salmon. At CVS, she'd peruse sale items as leisurely as we used to the handmade in those New England craft shops. Now it was Folger coffee, shampoo and vitamins. When we'd reach the feminine hygiene aisle, she'd shoo me away to go find her toothpaste, because she was embarrassed about her bladder leakage. And dumbfounded by the wide confusing assortment of pantie liners, so that when I returned too soon, she'd snap "Oh, *please*. You're rattling me!"

True. I *would* rattle her. Especially when I needed to account for the unaccountable, arriving on mornings when she'd spilled her coffee on the bed and we'd have to strip her sheets; when she had a doctor's appointment, and was still in her nightgown, clothes spread out across the bed as if trying to decide what to wear to art openings and out to dinner. Doctor appointments proved particularly problematic, because they were just that, appointments, that could be cancelled if we were fifteen minutes late.

On the morning of an appointment with her cardiologist, I arrived to find her moving haltingly around her room.

"Oh, why is it I can't find *anything* anymore..."

"Your cane?" I found it on the other side of the bed and quickly handed it to her.

"My *shoes*." Then something else caught her attention, and she settled heavily onto the bed. "Would the boys like these?" She dangled a sheet of polar bear stamps in front of me where I was crouching to peer under her bed for her shoes. No doubt she'd donated to some save-the-polar-bears fund. Although I had not yet taken away her checkbook, I'd begun to worry about that, the accumulating charitable "thank you" gifts that arrived in the mail; besides the stamps, totes, calendars, and giant calculators for the near-blind.

I found her shoes under her bed and tried to maneuver her arthritic feet into them.

"I can *do* that," she said, bending down in that way I hated; I was afraid she'd pop out the artificial ball from her hip. "This is what you always do. You *rush* me. It would be better if I just went by myself!"

"I'm not rushing you," I lied. It was painful watching her struggling to get on her own shoes. "We actually have a good half hour before we need to leave," I said cheerfully, my jaw starting to ache; I was clenching my teeth, something I thought I only did in my sleep.

"Why do we have to leave so early?" She looked at her watch. "The appointment's at one, isn't it? It's only ten."

"It's eleven *thirty*."

She squinted at the tiny roman numerals. "Oh, I think it's stopped."

I thought about what I'd get her for Christmas, a large-faced watch with big numbers.

"Mom, it's forty-five minutes away. We need to leave in *one half hour*."

"Well, I should just drive myself! You do not need to drive me!"

I felt as boxed in as a raging cat. We could argue about that, whether I needed to drive her. We'd be reduced to a battle of wills, until I convinced her she needed someone there to take notes; at least she could not refute *that* fact, her memory not what it used to be.

I knew to leave her alone, and I went into the kitchen to wash whatever dishes still in the sink from the night before (my mother saw no point in fixing the dishwasher since she'd "be gone soon, anyway."). I dried and returned them to the built-in hutch, next to my grandmother's yellow tea set no one was allowed to use, on display there for over thirty years. After my mother died, I'd find a sticky note in one of the cups, where she'd scrawled "DO NOT USE!" a warning to her last aide, the one who would move in.

The remnants of lentil soup were encrusted in a pot on the stove. On the kitchen table was a stack of mail, those charitable solicitations and more catalogues. My mother's life I imagined as one interrupted. She was easily distracted and would forget what she was doing, with vitamin pills left counted out on a dish; bills left opened but unpaid; miscellaneous numbers scribbled on various notepads. Then there was the miscellany that accumulated in various baskets or containers: an old wooden flatware holder on the table beside her bed housed nail files, her "Age Defying" neck cream, more stamps, key-chain flashlights, their batteries long since eroded. The brass cigarette holder I remember from my childhood, was jam-packed with safety pins, more nail files, combs, and the cat's nail clippers. Detritus that I would come to see as the residuals of old age, of a life now confined.

On the butcher's block was an open jar of marmalade and a package of English muffins, left there from the middle of the night when she was up, unable to sleep. After putting everything away, I took a sponge to scrub the dried warped wood. She once had taken such care of it, oiling it regularly. I scrubbed at the encrusted marmalade, leaning into the same pool of amber light from the overhead red lamp shade, as so many times before we had stood around that table—for the recurring, of my nieces and nephews visiting in the summer, when my mother would pack elaborate beach picnics. And for those pivotal moments that marked turning points in our lives; the night before my father went into the nursing home: "We've been a good family," my mother had said. My father had spread out his hands on the butcher's block, looking down at them, trying to hide his confusion. The next pivotal moment would come a good twenty years later, the night my mother was dying, when it would be my mother's doctor there, standing across from my mother's aide and me, instructing us on administering the morphine and liquid lorazepam.

Half an hour later, my mother still had not emerged from her bedroom. I was the one now looking at my watch —panic set in. I found her still sitting on the bed, transferring all her stuff from one purse to another—not even the handwoven one with the ceramic button, but one so old, I vaguely recognized it from when I was growing up. She had spread out her purse clutter across the bed, face powder, old tissues, crumpled supermarket receipts, lipsticks. A small note pad decorated with kittens.

"Mom, what are you *doing*?"

She opened her wallet, began taking out all her cards. "What is this AAA card? Do I still belong to that?"

"Mom, clean out your wallet later. We're only going to the doctor's." *We weren't going to an art opening or out to dinner.*

She looked at her watch again. "It's only ten."

"It's *noon*!"

"Noon? How can it be noon?" She put aside her emptied wallet to reset her watch again.

"You need a new battery."

She laughed. "And a new body."

I wasn't laughing. "We need to leave in five minutes."

"Well, I can't be ready in five minutes. Why didn't you tell me what time it was?"

I reminded myself not to clench my teeth.

I didn't want the appointment cancelled, as appointments could be, if we were late. There were those times when we arrived to have deadpan front-desk receptionists slide open their little glass partition long enough to tell us we'd have to reschedule. I held out her coat for her, resisting shoving her arms into the sleeves as I would the boys'.

"It *can't* be noon," she said, her voice shaking as it could when she coming undone, when she could cry, which only irritated me more.

"Your battery is *dead*!"

My mother went lax as a doll as I put her coat on.

I scooped up her purse contents as I would my boys' Legos, stuffed them into her beaded purse. I'd done it. I'd crossed that fine line I could teeter on precariously, that line between the daughter she still expected me to be and full mothering mode.

On the expressway, I drove 80. My neck craned, hands white on the wheel. My teeth clenched.

Usually, my mother would be checking herself in the overhead visor or rooting though her purse for a lipstick. This time she didn't check herself in the mirror. And neither was she close to tears. On this drive, she was stoic. She sat with her hands folded over that ancient purse.

We got there. I pulled into the handicapped spot.

"So what time is it now?" She asked, having given up on her own watch.

We were actually fifteen minutes early.

I felt foolish.

And exhausted.

She unfolded her hands from over her purse. I recognized it as a purse I'd once loved. One embroidered with tiny glass beads that she'd saved for special occasions, weddings, anniversaries, my father's faculty parties. As special as the purse may have been to her, she'd entrusted it to me for playing dress-up. I had modeled myself wearing it in front of a mirror. Pretending that I was her.

It was me now who was almost in tears. I wanted to lay my head on the steering wheel and blubber like a baby.

And she knew it.

"Take a breath," she said.

My mother could often say how sorry she was, as she had back in the emergency room. Now I was the one who wanted to say I was sorry.

I couldn't. And I didn't have to.

She took out a lipstick. She folded down the visor mirror. Not liking what she saw, she snapped it back up. "This too shall pass."

At the doctor's appointment, she would have an echocardiogram, and I'd witness the beating of my mother's heart. The results would only show mild calcification, which we already knew she had. But my own heart would quicken at the sight of my mother's, the fluttering of those black-and-white chambers. Quicken with fear, as when years earlier she'd been diagnosed with breast cancer, however early and ultimately curable. She'd undergone a mastectomy, and I'd come home to care for her while her incision healed. I remember how my hands shook when one night, I had to clear her drain of a blood clot, pinching it down the tube. She had spoken to me as calmly then as she did now. I don't think my mother any more really believed that "this too shall pass," but she could still say it for my sake.

7

My mother and doctors: she switched primary care physicians as frequently as hair stylists, rarely happy with the length or how they cut into her waves. These relationships would start off amicably enough: "Finally a doctor who will listen to me!" But the listening for my mother, unfortunately, was not so much about her ailments, as it was her broad-ranged, at times, sweeping frustrations, as if the mere venting might cure her of all her travails. Inevitably, these doctors seemed to stop listening, or at least from my mother's vantage point—I think they were still hearing her actual complaints, about her aching hip, acid reflux, arthritis, and insomnia. But finally, they could not measure up to her long-time doctor back when doctors could afford to spend time truly listening to their patients. Back when I was little and she was caring for her own mother, when she could "just stop in" for a B12 shot, when life's "pressures" became too much.

My mother's very last doctor before she died was Dr. Craig, whom she'd heard "great things about," whatever that meant. When it came time for her first appointment, she agreed to let me drive if I promised to let *her* do the talking. I admit, I could butt in, especially when she took the more circuitous rambling route which nearly always led off topic; I'd grown quite cognizant of that glazed look of doctors. Waiting for my mother *to get to the point*.

This time, we were actually on time, and the nurse ushered us into an airless room with one narrow window. A paper pink Venetian blind filtered in murky light. On one wall hung a reproduction of another window, this one overlooking a lush rose garden. The nurse helped my mother up the step to sit on the examining table, then sat at the computer and began rattling off the usual new-patient questions: had she'd ever had diabetes, cancer, thyroid, high blood pressure? And then: had she ever had any surgeries?

I thought about how many surgeries one person could rack up by age 90-something, and I didn't blame my mother for having to squeeze her eyes shut to remember them all.

"Well, I guess the first was having my tonsils out..."

Staring at the computer screen, the nurse could have been staring into an aquarium. "What year?"

"The year? Oh, I don't know I guess I was about eight..."

The nurse nodded. My mother's birthday was probably somewhere on the screen. She was doing the math.

"Any other surgeries?"

"Well, appendix after that I guess...."

"And when?"

"My mother opened her eyes. "You mean what year?"

"She was a child," I piped up.

My mother gave me a look.

"Any others? Surgeries?"

I could see that my mother was feeling overwhelmed, and to fill the long minutes as she shut her eyes again, I laughed, and then a bit too loudly said, "Well, there was your C-section, when you had me..."

The nurse was wearing a white blouse dotted with pink

flowers. That matched the walls. She didn't look at either of us, and I stared at the flowers. They started to have faces like little ghosts. "And when was that?" she asked.

"You really want me to remember the year?"

I couldn't help myself: "Um Mom...when I was born?"

My mother failed to see the irony. "Well, I realize that, just not what year."

"You had me when you were forty-five." I hoped the nurse would do the math, adding on the years to my mother's own birth year rather than mine. "1963."

Luckily, my mother then jumped ahead to her hip surgery, skipping over two hernias and her mastectomy, but then I wondered what the heck all this history mattered, except to fill in blanks on the screen.

"Hip replacement, and when was that?" the nurse asked.

My mother sounded exasperated. "Oh, I don't *know*, it was in the summer, and we were going to that restaurant, you know on east Main? That new restaurant that used to be called something or other but has always been changing hands...Anyway, they have these brick steps that are uneven..."

I began my deep breathing. This is the kind of digressing my mother always did. She couldn't seem to get past the fact that doctors don't care a hoot about the how or why. Just the what.

"2005," I piped up. Well, that was one I couldn't forget, the year Owen was born, when I was so engorged.

My mother glared at me.

The nurse wasn't looking at either of us. I watched her face in that watery computer glow, and she seemed elsewhere—away from this mother and daughter, turned inward toward her own travails, maybe a difficult morning with her own ornery mother or daughter.

"Medications?"

"Oh, goodness—the one for triglycerides, that's always been through the roof..."

"You happen to know the dose and name?'

"Lipitor, 40 mg," I said, opening my Big Black Bible to read it off my list.

"Perfect." The nurse now was looking at me. "Any others?"

I started to read off my nicely typed list until she asked if she could just copy them off the sheet.

The only sound in the airless pink room was the click of her maroon nails on the keyboard. My mother sat stock still, staring at the floor. I shifted my feet so my sneakers squeaked too loudly on the linoleum.

"So what brings you here today?" the nurse asked, her fingers poised over the keyboard.

"Why am I here? I'm looking for a doctor who will actually *listen* to me..."

The nurse now turned to my mother for the first time. She smiled wanly. "Any specific complaints?"

"I just don't feel good."

"Headaches? Stomach aches?"

"I'm *tired*. I'm tired and old, isn't that enough?"

The nurse cocked her head at the screen, clearly stymied as to how to fill in the blanks.

"Well, your wrist," I said. "You have trouble opening jars."

"Which wrist, right or left."

My mother wouldn't answer.

"Her right, isn't it, Mom?"

She stared stonily ahead at the roses out the fake window.

I stifled my rage at my mother's petulance.

"Ok, well..." The nurse slid off her stool. She seemed to chuckle a little then, as if she was used to seeing mothers and daughters spat in the tiny room. "Dr. Craig will be in shortly."

She left, shutting the door. I wish she'd left it open to let in some air into this airtight room.

My mother: "You make me look like a fool."

"You weren't answering her."

"I'm not an imbecile! And it's *my* body, I can speak for myself."

"Just saying you don't feel good isn't what they're looking for."

"You didn't give me a chance..."

"They don't need your whole life story, Mom..."

"I told you I should come alone."

I felt the pink walls closing in.

"Why do you always do that, take the other person's side? Why can't you just once take *my* side?"

I zeroed in on one perfect square in the mottled linoleum floor, resisted engaging in this taking-of-sides argument. Not taking my mother's side was a frequent grievance through the years. Any time I didn't agree with my mother, somehow, I was taking *sides*, and never hers. Though now I can wonder if it wasn't more about feeling overlooked than taking sides, a deep-rooted yearning for validation that resonated in those stories she would tell me again and again. I can't always remember the context of this retelling, but I do remember her tone, her frustration in the moment—with life's "pressures"—and doubting whether her work as an artist was finally "any good." She'd tell me again and again about her oldest brother Arthur dying from Streptococcus at seventeen—when she was only ten, and the minister failing to acknowledge my mother's presence. "It was like I didn't exist," she could say quite vehemently, when she told me how the minister only addressed her other two older brothers. So that I always envisioned them all together, seated side by side in some Victorian parlor; the minister tall and daunting, failing to acknowledge the shy little girl with the wide face and small pale blue eyes.

Those same brothers would spend the summer after Arthur died tooting around in their motorboat on Lake

Sunapee, while my mother set out alone in her rowboat to paint with her first oil set. When not adrift alone in some cove of water lilies as I can imagine her, she was typing those letters to her father I'd find in her attic, ones of deep longing, the fervent urgency of a young child left to navigate her own confusion and grief: "Oh! How you are missed, Daddy. I miss you terribly. Everything is lonely without you and so sad. Everything would be perfect if you were here." She'd write to her father about her practicing for the horse show, about her trotting and cantering, and about how otherwise, she was left alone afternoons to read a book while her mother played golf and her brothers were off aeroplaning: "If I did not have that rowboat, I'm sure I do not know what I would do for it would be so lonely." Again and again in those letters, there is yearning: "The salmon are missing your smelt, and the bass are missing your spinner to get mad at, so you should come up very soon. Please do for I miss you dreadfully." And I would imagine her again and again, the young girl with the wavy blond hair, typing alone in a cottage, maybe by an open window overlooking the lake.

This reverberation, this loneliness, I know weighed on my mother; nights when I was growing up back in the Staten Island house, I'd come downstairs to find her standing in a corner of the kitchen against the Formica counter, clutching a small glass of Scotch, contemplative in a way I rarely remember her except when she might be sitting in those cellar shadows, staring at an unfinished canvas. As if thinking back to the way things were, puzzling over how things might have been: about her own mother who hadn't been able to understand the "Night Garden," the flowers largely obscured in darkness except for one brilliant pink one; about her brothers who would always treat her like a baby sister; and finally, about her daughter, who never took her side. After she died, I'd find a scribbled list of New Year's resolutions which included "not to be so hurt by Sandy." I'd refold it to tuck back where I'd found it, inside a jewelry box, amongst the rectangular soldered nail bracelets she'd always worn.

I was glad when the doctor came in—a breath of fresh air in that stifling room. As if she were just stopping in for tea, she breezed over to my mother, introducing herself with a strong handshake. She settled herself on the stool as if she had all the time in the world, not a waiting room full of impatient waiting patients. And so my mother launched into a long-winded story about how she'd left one doctor or another, and they began to chat like old friends when Dr. Craig mentioned she'd run into one of these numerous doctors, retired now, at local 5K races she often ran weekends in town.

I sat in my chair against the wall, feeling like a child who should not interrupt the grown-ups, should most definitely be seen and not heard.

"So what brings you here today?" She finally asked.

"Oh, well plenty of things. My daughter thinks I can carry on."

Dr. Craig gave me a cursory glance as if only now noticing the grown child in the room.

"Well, you're 92." She gave my mother's knee a brief, gentle squeeze. "I would say you've earned your right to carry on!"

They laughed for a bit, and my mother gave me one of her "I told you so" looks, that brief raise of her eyebrows. I was angry then that she could make me feel this: shamed. But also grateful to this doctor for her kindness and congeniality—a gratefulness that would extend quite literally to my mother's dying day, when Dr. Craig would make her last home visit to my mother, confined by then, to that hospital bed. Dr. Craig would look down into my mother's face as if to memorize her. My mother, in the throes of dementia, would forget how grateful she herself had been, and would tell her "I think you're just awful."

Dr. Craig would only smile, tenderly brush back a wisp of my mother's white hair. She would help my mother's aide to change the sheets, as my mother's body, she explained, had begun to "clean itself out." Donning latex gloves, she would handle my mother with the same tenderness and respect as this first time they met, one that still resonates with me all these years later.

8

Sometimes I can wonder how things might have been if my father were still alive. If my parents had been able to grow old together, to hold hands on walks like my mother's elderly neighbors whom she could envy. The truth is, my mother and I were an anomaly—there was something about the placement of us in my father's life that we never quite fit properly. He was already 63 when I was born, in between the births of his third and fourth grandchild—there's a photo of my father sitting on the lawn with my sister, her with a new toddler, my father with his new baby; we would all grow up close enough in age for us to play together, to sit in a row in matching orange life jackets on my half-sister's sailboat. I would forever be the relative everyone was always trying to figure out how they were related to, and I would refer to my nieces and my nephew as cousins—easier than trying to explain that I was their aunt before I was born.

My father, a historian, and already planning his retirement after almost 40 years of teaching history, certainly hadn't seen himself becoming a father all over again in his sixties. He perhaps saw himself writing more books, once he finished his last, on the Wilke's expedition, one my mother helped him research on their honeymoon.

My mother would tell the story of my birth; how the police had to wake my father up, as he'd gone back to bed after dropping my mother at the hospital, and slept so soundly, he didn't hear the phone ring. But there is a photo of him holding me as a newborn, cradling me in one crooked elbow, so that he is able to look me squarely in the face—he's smiling, clearly pleased by this newfound fatherhood. I am looking up at him at once astonished and enraptured.

My earliest memories of my father are of mutual adoration. He would hold me on his lap so I could bang on his Royal typewriter, pressing the bright red button to make the lid spring up. Those summers in Vermont, daily we motored over to Bird's store for the mail and Bazooka bubble gum he'd buy for me; I can see him, the way he handled the small outboard motor like a tamed beast—I was otherwise terrified of thing, with its long cord he'd yank powerfully. Then there are photos of those moments I don't remember, but can imagine: of him first pushing me down the hill in our backyard on my little wooden go-cart with the orange wheels; then me pushing *him* down the hill on that same tiny cart, his knees tucked up under his chin, both of us laughing. Up in Vermont, my father and I are wading into the lake. Our backs are to the camera, as it must have been my mother who snapped the picture; I'm swirling the skirt of my yellow and white bathing suit in the water, watching my father wetting his arms first before diving in. I can imagine a moment later, my mother putting down the camera on the arm of one of the cedar Adirondack chairs, plowing past us into the water, yelling, "Ooooh, you're doing it the *hard* wayyyy!" Leaving us in her wake.

More vivid and tactile are the uncomfortable moments between us, and there are exactly two. The first one was when he hit a dog on the way back from picking me up from school when I was in sixth grade. I remember the drive as eternal, from the second the dog flew off in slow motion from the right front bumper to land somewhere behind us.

I cannot say what kind of dog it was. I remember it as a gray blurry shadow. But the impact was pronounced. A dull and definitive thud that I both heard and felt.

My father did not slow down.

"Daddy!"

He looked nervously in his rearview mirror.

I pleaded with him to go back. "Daddy, you hit a *dog*!"

"There's nothing we can do about it now..." he said, tentatively.

I know I was crying. Though perhaps silently, as I too did not want to go back.

We did not speak. My father did that thing he would do, just lifting his one hand from the wheel as if obsessively checking the gas gauge.

When we pulled into the driveway, I got out, slamming the door. I ran in to find my mother.

When I told her what happened, she seemed less upset by the fact that my father hit a dog in the first place, than by him leaving without finding its owner. She went outside, yelling "David! That's someone's *dog*!"

I don't remember if my father had even gotten out of the car, before my mother was already getting into it. He did not argue about their going back to the spot where my father hit the dog. I watched from the safety of my window seat, glad to be left behind, ensconced in the stillness of the house, even if I didn't like particularly to be left alone.

The dog was still there, dead in the road, and they would eventually find out it was a stray, but not before knocking on all the doors on the street. Rather, I imagine my father waited in the car, or if he did accompany my mother, he moved far more slowly, lingering perhaps, on the walkways—there is no doubt in my mind that it was my mother who rang the doorbells or banged brass knockers, throwing herself into this ugly task as she would plunge into the lake's cold water.

The one other uncomfortable moment was the only time I remember my father trying to break through what had become a hazy screen hanging between us. I was angry about something he did or didn't do, when he followed me into my room after I'd slammed the door.

He stood there, on the other side of my twin bed; not quite coming in to sit and talk, not something he ever would have done. His hands fell open in a kind of supplication at his sides, and he asked, "Do you resent me because I'm an old fellow?"

An old *fellow*. The phrasing of this question for forty-odd years has been emblazoned in my memory. As if in the asking he was already wishing to withdraw his question, a spear now through that hazy screen, even with the masking of old "father" with the lighter of "fellow." Clearly, he knew how much I hated that he was already retired, that he had enough time to leisurely wheel himself around on that old orange-wheeled go-cart to weed the front walk. He knew how much I resented him for being old. How I would never be able to think about him ever having been young, until after his death, when we came across pictures of him with his basketball team or college fraternity. When I'd see there a virility I'd glimpsed as a little girl but long since had lost sight of in the old man.

The room felt close as if all the windows were tight shut. Sweltering with our grim silence. Shadows of the trees outside darted frantically across my daisy wallpaper.

I flushed with embarrassment. And shock—at the first time feeling cowed by my father. "No...." I stammered. And remained standing there, on the other side of my bed with my baby dolls and Snoopy a cluttered mess on my pillow.

My father smiled a little, as if he too now was embarrassed. He left, his hands still hanging open. I heard the creak of the old floorboards as he walked slowly down the hall to his dusty office.

That is what I always thought, that I'd resented him because he was old. I worried my peers might think this slightly stooped white-haired man picking me up from school might be my *grand*father. But I can wonder whether my resentment was finally less about his being older, than about his nature; I can wonder if his relationship with my half-sister, Catharine, had been any different. As I can wonder whether his marriage to my mother was one of real love, more than an aberration after his life-path was derailed by the death of his first wife—I will never know the story of this first youthful romance for my father. How deeply or not the loss of this woman may have fractured him, followed some years later, by the death of his firstborn daughter.

I remember knowing my half-sister Catharine was going to die long before I realized my father seemed not to. I knew what my mother seemed to know, when we first heard that her breast cancer had returned. We were up in Vermont and one night, after we'd all gone to bed, I overheard her say to my father, "Oh, David I'm so *sorry*..."

She spoke softly, her voice almost lost against the lapping of the waves through my open window. I waited for my father to say something. There was only the sound of lightning bugs striking the screen.

What would follow was a year of frustrations as my mother felt we should be doing more for Catharine, though what exactly I don't know. What she maybe was facing up to better than my father could, was the looming reality that soon my nieces and nephew, two still in their teens, would be losing their mother. And she wanted to fix it. To somehow make it right, face it head on much as she had banging on those doors.

Shortly before my sister died, I overheard my mother pleading with my father: " She's dying, David. We should be *doing* something..."

And my father's reaction: "You don't *know* she's dying..."

Catharine died two months later. I think about the last time my father ever saw his daughter. Catharine had invited us all over for a visit, but I refused to go. I made up some excuse, of having to study for finals, as maybe I was retreating into my own denial; my mother would tell me how Catharine baked them cookies and told them that she'd reserved her burial plot in Greenwood Cemetery, where her mother was buried and where my father would be laid to rest.

It was almost a year to the day since her recurrence when she died, and we were up in Vermont again, when we heard the news.

We did not have a phone, so one day we received a telegram delivered to Bird's store. We went next door to the neighbor's, and I remember it was my mother on their phone, a wall one in the kitchen, pulling the cord out into the hall where my father and I huddled. She started to cry on the phone: "I'm so, so sorry..." And then me: I ran out of the house painted a green to blend into the dense trees, back through the crooked path to our barn-red house, back into full sun, unable to stop my own tears. Probably regretting that I hadn't seen my half-sister when I had the chance before she died, when she made those sugar cookies.

I don't remember how my father responded, though I know he did not cry. I can imagine him locked into a moment where he could only sit on their hall chair, and look at his hands. But the air that day no doubt hung heavy; the quiet and stillness of the lake oppressive. My mother got us up and moving, quite literally, if only to drive off somewhere, into town.

After my father died, my mother would find in the attic a box of postcards that he'd written to her before they were married; he had proposed and was awaiting an answer, as he was travelling while doing research on his second book. They were postcards that seemed to surprise and sadden my mother. They surprised her because, in my father's tiny cramped script, they expressed a breadth of feeling that otherwise in their thirty years together, he seemed unable to express. And they saddened her, I think, because my mother felt cheated of what they might have been, if she hadn't spent the first half of her marriage living in another woman's house, in the shadow of a first wife he would be buried next to.

The second half of her marriage she spent caring for my father as his mind went, until he no longer could distinguish between times of day, and my mother put him in the nursing home. The first time my mother and I visited my father, he tried to leave with us through the automated glass doors. I remember him in only an undershirt. Maybe he had taken off his shirt in distress, as sometimes he could start to take off his pants because he was convinced that they belonged to someone else. But there was my father, uncharacteristically asserting himself by pushing past a nurse to follow us down the pastel hallway. Before he could make it to the automatic doors, the nurse was able to redirect him back to the cafeteria, and I imagine once we were out of his line of sight, he forgot that we had been there at all.

My mother did not forget. Once the doors shut behind us, she lifted her hands to her temples, as if she could physically block out this new reality. She couldn't. "This is *awful*," she exhaled, as if she'd truly been holding her breath, tears welling up—she blinked hard, to clear her vision.

The next time we visited my father, he already had a girlfriend—we arrived to find them sitting side by side in hall, holding hands. "We are happy today because David had a huge bowel movement!" The lady in thick glasses exclaimed, grinning with this marvelous news.

My father laughed, not at all embarrassed, as if he'd been granted some kind of award, at once immensely proud and his usual modest self. But I don't think from the time those glass doors locked behind us, my mother could see past her regret to what may have been fact: my father was content. His natural disposition was to look past the painful, to where he could find a reprieve, which now might be holding hands with a stranger, or honing in on a drawing behind the nurse's station with the markers my mother had brought him. Away from the grief of losing his first wife, then his first-born daughter. Away even from hitting a stray dog. To what was in front of him, a blank sheet of paper and an array of colorful markers; my mother gave him a sketchbook, and he filled it with drawings of owls, flowers and sailboats, two little men fishing, their boat casting a fine pink and yellow shadow, though he rarely filled a page, except for one of a large sprawling bird in full flight. She wrote on the cover the number of his room, his name in big block letters and "Please give to David his colored *PENS* to draw with."

Years later, when my mother descended into her own truly dark and terrifying dementia, I would consider my father quite lucky—except for the day he was actively dying, when he thrashed against the inevitable, I don't remember a single day in his life of true angst.

Occasionally, I made the visits to my father by myself, and in the privacy of my notebook, I began to write him letters in a way I'd never actually been able to talk to him, not even that day when I'd had the chance, when he'd confronted me about being an old fellow. I wrote about my visiting him a week before his 93rd birthday, his last, when I drove him to one of our favorite spots, a small pier overlooking a grassy inlet. I gave him one of his birthday presents, a box of chocolates, and he told me he'd forgotten his age, but perhaps he was around seventeen. "Seventeen?" I echoed.

He thought for a long moment, then said, "No, I think I'm 21."

A flock of mallards lazily circled the end of the pier where a family was crabbing, dangling chicken wings into the water at the end of fishing lines. The children excitedly paced back and forth, tugging on their lines to check their tautness, and my father thought it was the ducks they were trying to catch. Biting into a cream-filled candy, he wondered whether the ducks wouldn't prefer chocolate. "I wouldn't mind being a duck for a day," he added. "To have so many feathers, you could swim in all kinds of weather."

"I wouldn't mind either," I said. "To be a duck for a day."

As we sat there, he made the same observations over and over, and I allowed myself to become caught up in the flow of his repetitions. When he remarked again and again on the duck's feathers, I answered again and again how I wouldn't mind being a duck for a day.

A child pulled up a nibbled chicken wing, and when my father wondered whether it wasn't for the ducks, I suggested they might prefer chocolate. That afternoon, I began to see what I had gained, what had been laid bare by his dementia—a new, more open access to what had always been there. I got caught up in the moment as I hadn't since I was a little girl, when he would point out to me the thin tail of a cloud left by a plane.

Two months later, my father collapsed and never walked again. This most likely was the progression of his Alzheimer's but my mother saw it as neglect on the part of the facility; she had him moved to another nursing home closer to us, so that she could visit more often, until she was truly strung out and exhausted. Soon after my father stopped walking, he stopped talking, though he would smile and laugh silently as if telling himself jokes. Then, he would gesticulate with his hands as if having something urgent to say, and my mother and I would lean into him, only to hear him whisper little nonsensical nothings.

It was around this time when my mother bought him a teddy bear.

I was aghast. "You bought Daddy a stuffed *animal*?"

"It will comfort him," she said, though my father did not seem as distraught as we'd become. I don't know if the bear comforted him, but he surely loved it, would play with it on his wheelchair tray, making it hop like a bunny. All my old resentments over the years didn't exactly melt away, but experiencing my father in such a vulnerable state, I felt for him. I made the bear's paws clap. My father laughed his wide silent laugh so that his gold fillings gleamed.

One day, a month before he died, my father did speak again. It was Valentine's Day, and we'd brought him cards and chocolates that would melt safely in his mouth. We stood the cards up on his wheelchair tray—my mother's, one of a couple inside a heart, holding hands like they never did, with something about love as eternal as the ocean tide—and he kept looking from one to the other, as enraptured as a child by the bright colors, and the pop-up heart. My mother asked, "David, what can we get you?"

Anxious to do more.

He smiled, held out his hands. "I have all I need!" he said, gesturing at the array of cards as if at a big wide wonderful world.

My father died when I was 30, soon after my first novel *Blue Glass* was published. I brought it to show him in the nursing home and sat beside him on the bed to show him the book. He turned it over and over in his hands like some box he couldn't figure out how to open. I reminded him what I knew he'd forgotten, that I was a writer, and now I was an author like he was. I'd inscribed the book to him, even though I knew he'd never read it. It would be forgotten on his bedside table by the time I left, the cover stained with a ring from his juice cup with the pink straw.

When the nurses cleaned out his room, the book was returned to us mixed in with the maroon sweater he always wore, his drawings, the stuffed bear, and the vibrant red Valentine Day cards. I would place it beside his own two books on the living room shelf. My father, the maritime historian, who spent years of his life immersed in the history of another, Charles Wilkes who spent years at sea. Who clearly found refuge in the past. Before *The Wilke's Expedition*, he wrote a book about the Delaware River. One book was dedicated to his first wife, the second to my mother. And each in the singular: "For my wife."

For him, unlike for my mother when she died, I cried copiously. Real tears. My mother on the other hand, had already experienced real losses in her life, of both her parents, as well as two brothers, so part of her got caught up in the things that needed to be done. She was able to quickly toss his clothes into plastic bags to give away, which seemed ruthless to me until I was the one doing the same with her own clothes—the only way I could part with the intimate was *quickly*. I would see it for what it was, her trying to move past her own pain, the way she had put her hands up to her temples when those glass doors had locked behind us.

9

There was a time when it was my mother who drove that stretch of highway between our two points on the map. She loved that drive, especially during opera season, when she'd blast live Metropolitan performances from national public radio. As she pulled into our driveway, I could hear some aria reverberating through her car as it used to through our house when I was growing up, when she'd blast it from both the cellar and the living-room stereos. If it was Puccini's *Madame Butterfly*, and I came down to her studio, she'd wave me off with a paint brush.

It was often dusk when she arrived. By the time she got "the cats settled" with clean litter pans and numerous Purina Cat Chow bowls and her various "catch-all" bags packed—the free ones from L'Oreal where she'd shop at Macy's for her makeup—it was late afternoon, and she would be driving west, into the setting sun. "Oh you should've seen the sky. It was *gorgeous*!" she'd exude, describing the colors of magenta and phthalo blue as if she were already painting it in her mind, and I'd tell her that I'd begun to worry. "Don't be such a worrier," she'd say, when increasingly I *would* worry, about her driving, and eventually, I bought her a flip phone. One time she called me because she somehow took a wrong turn. This was before Google Maps, and she could not tell me where she was. "I have *no idea* where I am," she cried, clearly frustrated, but a little exhilarated. "But I'll figure it out." She hung up, and I stayed by the window until I finally saw her pull into our driveway.

When the boys were very little, my mother drove up most holidays. At Easter, she would arrive with egg coloring kits, and sit at the kitchen table to help the boys scribble on the eggs with wax crayons, then dip them into the dies, encouraging them to try all the different colors. At Christmas, it was shopping bags of presents for the boys, some as carefully wrapped as she used to wrap my own, with decorative tags cut from old Christmas cards with pinking shears, and bows with pine cones and holly from her backyard. Every year, she drove down to Sag Harbor to buy them each an ornament from her favorite shop. The first Christmas after she died, the boys did their real grieving as they unwrapped those ornaments, the snowman on a unicycle, Santa pulling a red wagon. And always, she drove up for the boys' birthday parties. Before resorting to catalogues, she bought their presents from another favorite store, a toy shop in Southampton. She was there on the mornings of their birthdays, when they woke to birthday tables decorated as elaborately as my mother used to decorate for my own birthdays when I was a child.

The boys delighted in Gramma arriving in her old blue dodge van, and they'd help her carry in the various little bags packed with shoes, pill bottles, and little treats for them from her Five & Dime store, a set of jacks, water guns, or new gel pens. She'd sit on a chair in the playroom as they showed her their latest Lego creations and I realize now what a large presence she was in their young lives. She'd effuse over their drawings as she always had my own, on paper napkins when I'd color in the tiny embossed flowers. Her exuberance resonated with them, and they'd settle down to draw for her more giant spiders, giraffes, and dragons, while she'd encourage them to fill up the whole page.

But in *my* house, I wanted to command my own space as much as my mother did in her "happy house." Up nights, now in *my* kitchen, she left her opened English muffin packages and marmalade jars. She'd leave her tea mugs and tissues lying around the house, reorganize my pots and pans: "If you just stacked them, you'd have so much more *space*." She'd empty my linen closet to refold my sheets: "If only you didn't just throw things in there." She'd soak my refrigerator bins and empty the dishwasher's silverware baskets to separate the dirty forks and knives: "They will be so much easier to put away!" I might come down in the middle of the night to find her digging out the grime between the backsplash and counter in our old Formica kitchen with a paring knife.

It was easier to be her daughter in her own home, than in mine where I was first and foremost, a mother. If you look up the definition of mother, you will find references to not just child bearing, child rearing, but to exercising control, influence, and authority. Or maybe I was even *more* daughter, in that way I could bristle; in a way I should have rebelled back when I was a teenager, when all my friends were rebelling against their mothers by lying about being at someone else's house when they were really hanging out at the mall. Goodness knows, I could slam my door on her as I might have on my father, when she denied me something I deemed crucial to my teen sustenance, caramel vinyl Go-Go boots she told me were "cheap looking." Because why would I want to go and wear such ugly boots that made me look *cheap*? And then there were those darker moments between us, the night I held a knife to my mother's throat—granted, a dull old dinner knife if not a butter one. But my mother pushed back her head, thrust out her throat and said, "Well, go ahead. Do it then." I have no memory of what I was so angry about that I wanted to kill my mother, only the fury of the moment, then the deflation of it as she knew I would never be able to slit her throat—she knew this too would "pass."

No doubt, I slammed down the knife and went off to slam my door. And my fury could certainly be met by her own, from her emptying all my bureau drawers into a pile in the middle of my green shag rug when I refused to clean my room, to her cornering me when I had a boyfriend to visit, one who boasted large thick-braided gold chains and lay out on my mother's deck with his hairy chest slick with suntan oil. She let me know in no uncertain terms that he was little better than a gigolo, and I met her disgust with a spitting anger; more so because she saw what I would discover, but before she gave me a chance to see it for myself. Still, for most of my life, I would think of my mother and me as having been close, though not in the way some might still say of us—not necessarily as best friends or sisters, assuming we shared our innermost secrets, which we didn't. What they are acknowledging is something else entirely; a closeness based not on familial kinship or unconditional trust. Not even on that closeness of the circumstantial, of our being that anomaly in my father's life. What my mother and I had was something more integral than an allegiance—something inherent in both our dispositions, in our very makeup. A driving force that, time and again, despite our self-doubts, propelled us back to the blank page or canvas.

But under my own roof, in my own house, where I was learning what it meant to command my own space as mother, I was finally learning what it really meant as a daughter, to say no.

"You don't have to be so difficult," she said. She had wanted to buy me a new couch.

It was the day after Christmas, when we made our annual shopping excursion to Ikea, and where she could insist on buying me things *she* felt I needed for the house: new pot holders (admittedly, mine were stained and burnt);

measuring spoons (I only had the nesting type); soup bowls, juice glasses, a new cutting board. For the most part, I accepted these gifts. But on the last Ikea trip we ever took, she was intent on that new couch. Our old one, she rightly argued, was uncomfortable, and the cream upholstery was stained with chocolate hand prints.

"You really need a new couch," she said sitting on one in the Ikea couch department, happy I think, to be able to sit at all.

I didn't need a new couch. If only because she was insisting that I did. But also because thinking couches wasn't something I could do just then; Christmases had become exhausting. My mother no longer was able to drive herself up to see us. So I had driven out Christmas Eve day to pick her up and be back in time for the boys to play shepherds in the church pageant. Various amalgams of sweaters and shawls were spread out across her bed, as she couldn't decide what to pack. She still insisted on wrapping the boys' presents, even though she had trouble with her arthritic hands; I found her near tears in the corner room, unable to get the tape dispenser to work. I didn't have the boys with me, as my husband had the day off, but even so, we barely made it back in time for them to change into their shepherd costumes.

"Just *try* this one." She patted the seat beside her on the couch. "Though not with these of course," she said, dismissing the zebra print pillows flanking her.

I came and stood in front of her. She seemed out of place between the zebra pillows. "No."

She gave me a look I knew too well. When I was being "difficult."

"I'm *not* buying a new couch today."

I was unreasonably angry, because I was tired. And preoccupied with my own worry that my mother might have another fall, right there in the couch department in the middle of sprawling Ikea. I imagined her falling and breaking her other hip, of EMS workers having to navigate a stretcher through the endless, IKEA winding aisles. And for a split moment I didn't care—long enough to watch her struggle, as she tried to get up off the couch, before I put out my arm to help her.

The last time I remember my mother staying with us, was after that fall when she fell into her television and suffered "chest contusions"—a euphemism for painful-as-hell bruised ribs. After a day in the emergency room, I drove her back to our house, in only her nightgown and nonskid hospital socks. It was a Sunday, and the boys did not seem particularly phased by Gramma arriving without a suitcase and in only a nightgown; they gave her big hugs, and Owen showed her how he'd learned to kick a small rubber ball off his heel to catch in one hand.

Having her stay the weekend while I could secure an aide for her recovery back home, I thought made sense. But I had another reason: Lucas had an ortho appointment first thing Monday morning, one I already had postponed several times due to my mother's other emergencies.

I remember less my mother's actual visit than the time I spent worrying about her while we were at the orthodontist. The ortho technician was displaying in her palm a tiny blue ring. To demonstrate its extraordinary flexibility, she squeezed it between two fingers. She explained how these "spacers" would be placed between my eight-year-old's teeth, to force spaces required to fit his expander. Lucas had a crossbite. (I had yet to digest that the expander would be a monstrous metal plate glued to the roof of his mouth.)

I stared at the tiny-blue-ringy-spacer thing, trying to focus on this ortho demonstration, when all I could think about was my mother: I'd left her on our futon lounge chair back at the house. "I'll be fine," she'd said. She'd just visited the bathroom and I'd left her lunch tray beside the lounge so there was really no reason she would have to get up before we returned to the house—which she couldn't, anyway, not without help. It would have perhaps made more sense for her to lie on the relatively high platform bed in the guest room, but then she'd have to navigate going up the stairs which by itself was an ordeal. We'd settled on the lounge chair which she found the most comfortable, anyway: "This is *so* comfortable!"

The technician continued to take out things to display: a box of fake teeth. A fake upper jaw with the monstrous metal expander thing glued to it.

This casual little lesson was all meant to make my son feel more comfortable. He stared wide-eyed, barely breathing.

I stared wide-eyed as well, though was envisioning my mother on the lounge chair. Suddenly having to get up.

Lucas was then directed to sit in a dental chair, and we waited for the orthodontist. Who then showed us the scans of Lucas's skull, and even his neck and vertebrae.

"You have a ginormous brain," Owen said. "And extremely long teeth."

I wished now that Owen hadn't tagged along. Though, of course, I couldn't have left him home alone with his grandmother, could imagine my mother convincing him to help her get up by her leaning on his little shoulder until they toppled over into a single mangled heap.

Lucas didn't speak, lost in awe and confusion at the site of his own skull, jaw and vertebrae. Otherwise, I'm sure he would have called his little brother a numbskull.

The doctor explained that he could set the mold for Lucas's teeth right then and there, because it would take only 20 minutes.

Twenty minutes! A long time when you've left your elderly mother on a lounge chair she cannot get off of by herself.

My daughterly intuition set in and I said we would have to reschedule for another visit. That we needed to go. *Now*.

I raced home.

Risking a ticket was a good thing; I got home just as my mother was trying to leverage herself up off the lounge chair to go to the bathroom. Which she couldn't. If she moved the slightest wrong way, she was in acute pain.

"I really have to use the *john*." She held out her hand to me as if I could just pull her upright, which I couldn't without her screaming in pain.

I didn't know what to do.

Until I thought to move my son's keyboard bench over to the lounge.

Ten minutes of gentle maneuvering, and she was on the bench.

But it was still too low for her to be able to stand upright without pain.

"Oh, I *do* need to go..."

Think, think, think.

I spied my office stool. the one that swiveled up and down.

I wheeled that over. After another full fifteen minutes, I was able to slide her onto it. Then swivel it up to full height so that with my support, she could leverage herself up to a standing position.

We made a turtle race to the bathroom. Just in time.

There are always crises in motherhood. The first, when Owen at age three sliced open his foot on the heating baseboard. But I wasn't prepared for this, what it now meant to be a middle-aged mother with an aging mother of my own, in my own house. Where I had to remember I was a mother too–reminded by Owen who watched the whole episode from his perch on the stairs, waiting for Gramma to come out of the bathroom so he could show her a trick.

"Bet you can't do this, Gramma," he said when she finally emerged.

He made as if he could slide his thumb on and off.

She smiled, masking her pain. "That's *amazing!*"

10

I was perhaps never more wholly my mother's daughter than when we went clothes shopping, or rather, universally how I imagined mothers and daughters. I would not think about this until after she died, when I would be clothes shopping alone, and become acutely aware of some teenage daughter modelling a pretty rose-patterned dress she'd slipped over her head for her mother; or the sixty-odd year old woman with her mother in a wheelchair, holding up a blouse so her mother could reach up to feel the material. I was aware of this, daughters turning to their mothers as they would, or had, all of their lives, from the time when it was expected that mothers would take their young daughters shopping for school clothes and each summer season, bathing suits—how I remember my mother, when she would hold up some item still on its hanger, imagining how it might hang on my small frame, when I was too young to consider my mother anything other than what she'd always been, a pillar of strength and security. A careful nurturer of my own still developing fragile sense of self.

My mother picked out my clothes for as long as I can remember. After she died, I'd find some of my first dresses, the red and orange plaid I remember from my first day of kindergarten, mixed in with material scraps from when she sewed, as if she'd planned to cut them up for a patchwork quilt; even one she had made for me, a calico blue and yellow—I recognized it from one of those photos that had surfaced in her house, of me around age ten, posing out on our back patio on Staten Island. In another snapshot: I'm wearing the cream-colored dress with a macramé rose at the collar for the Junior prom. When I got engaged, she was the one to find my wedding dress, in a local Hamptons boutique, to call and tell me she'd found exactly what I'd been looking for.

At T.J. Maxx, she had the patience to comb through racks upon racks of random sweaters, tops, skirts, I didn't have. The last time we shopped there, dementia had not yet set in, but her balance by then was precarious, and she used a shopping cart for support while filling it with clothes for me.

My mother held up to my waist a mini skirt I would never wear, then put it back on the rack. "It's time you bought a girdle."

She was known not to mince words.

All I knew of girdles were her own I'd glimpsed as a little girl, impossibly complicated contraptions, thick-padded ivory-colored things, with all those little hanging straps and clips. "I don't think they make girdles anymore."

"Well, something for tummy control."

I felt suddenly depleted. "I hardly eat."

"It's not about eating, Dear. It's about age." She patted her own stomach, what she called her rubber tire. "There just comes a time."

A time. There were those earliest adolescent times: the discrete pink box of feminine necessities my mother mail-ordered, and with great expectancy I kept hidden beneath my bed; my first bra after my mother took note of my

breasts budding beneath my skimpy smock 70's blouses; my first deodorant and Daisy leg razors.
"Why don't you go get that done now."
"Get what done?"
"The girdle. A good one. Go to the underwear department."
The underwear department? Would I have to wade through intricate racks and racks of under things, which I enjoyed even less than racks and racks of mismatched clothes? The truth was, I wasn't ready for *this* particular time—a rite of passage far on the other side of adolescence. On that other, however meandering, descending one of middle age.
"I don't think they sell girdles at T. J. Maxx."
"Well, go and try these on then," she said, of the shopping cart full of clothes.
"In a dressing room?"
She laughed. "Yes, a *dressing room*. You won't be able to tell properly whether they fit."
I don't think I'd stepped into a dressing room since my first C-section, when my wardrobe was whittled down to spit-stained T-shirts and stretch pants. Since birthing two babies, chasing them down through toddlerhood and now picking up after them, I'd developed a true distaste for dressing rooms.
I'd forgotten how god-awful glaring dressing room lighting was. Casting the starkest shadows to accentuate every wrinkle and bulge. But there I found myself, walled in by mirrors and florescent lights, with mother—She came right in, relieved to sit down on the dressing room bench.
She handed me a too-slim sweater dress. "This would be very becoming on you."
I frowned at her.
"Oh, try it on. You've always had the figure. You just need some tummy control."

When my mother found my wedding dress in the Hamptons boutique, it was not at all the far more understated A-line with a bodice of fine vintage off-white lace I'd envisioned for myself. She insisted I take a train out from the city to see the dress, an A-line and with a lace bodice, but of bold brilliant white lace, and with a matching veil that sat like a small crown on my head: "Oh, but it's a *look*, Sandy. You look stunning!" she'd said, to my regal reflection in the large boutique mirror, and I was beholden to her as I'd always been, for the way she could see me as I couldn't see myself. I was swept up in her enthusiasm as when shopping at Bloomingdales for my freshman year at college, what seemed hours we spent in the dressing room, my mother handing me hangers of skirts and blouses. Her looking at me in the mirror in her appraising way, crinkling her nose in dislike: "Too nambypamby." The namby-pamby would be something I had selected, some "droopy" skirt or top, and I'd take it off. I'm sure we left that day with other clothes, but what I remember is my mother's exuberance over the concert of elements she no doubt orchestrated: the wool skirt, a longsleeved blouse with a high, quite regal, collar, and a shimmering velvet black-and-eggplant vest. Walled in together as we were by the dressing room mirrors, I can see her now, giving a little clap of excitement and exclaiming "Oh, you are *stunning*!"

Contemplating me in those mirrors, my mother could always see me as I could never see myself. And there I was again, stripping down to my bra and underwear, feeling no less self-conscious than when I'd tried on that skirt and blouse before my college freshman year. Or my wedding dress.

I was surprised my mother didn't remark on at least my old worn bra, sagging where it should be showing more support, but she was intent now on my pending transformation—I slipped the sweater dress over my head.

My mother smiled. I didn't see her smile much those days. "*Look* at you."

She got up from the bench with surprising ease, energized now; she came over to adjust the dress around my shoulders, pull at it so it sat just right around my waist.

Even now, I can stand in front of a dressing room mirror, gazing at my own furrowed expressions, turning this way and that, and have no idea whether I really look good or not. I may not have been able to share my mother's same exuberance, but I had faith in the promise it held. She could anticipate my future in a way I never could, with expectation rather than trepidation, of exploring foreign rocky roads and riding horses down mountains in thunderstorms.

The truth is, on that rocky road in New Mexico, I had only felt that, trepidation—the part of me that would have hung back like my father, from knocking on all those doors. While my mother was reveling in the light and landscape, my chest was tightening with the "what ifs," as I obsessively checked the gas gauge. "You're *afraid* of life, aren't you?" I remember her saying to me one night, years later, over several glasses of wine at dinner. Whatever we had been talking about, I must have betrayed my timidity. And in her remark there was epiphany. As if in all those moments of her contemplating me in mirrors, she had only been looking at a mirage. But also compassion: she could not bear for me not to live my life to its fullest.

11

From the time my boys were babies, every summer we rented a house on a lake, and my mother would come up with us. The draw of lake settings had always been a deeply personal one for us both, and on those New England trips, we could seek out waterfront inns. My own memories of our summers on the Vermont lake are the most sensory of my childhood: the creak of the old springs on the screen door; my father cranking up the wood stove on cold mornings; the light the refrigerator cast across the rafters on nights when my mother was up, the gentle slap of her cards on the vinyl tablecloth as she played solitaire. For my mother, those Vermont summers she spoke of as her happiest—a reprieve from "life's pressures," where we spent our days at the lake's edge, my father reading in an Adirondack chair, my mother whiling away mornings on the dock with her coffee pot and newspaper. What I remember best is her sketching, and after she died, I would find sketchbooks filled with pen drawings of the birch trees, ferns and old stumps; a few of myself, sitting in the Adirondack chair, my hair in pigtails, changing the dress on my Barbie doll. Some sketchbooks are interspersed with my own drawings, those quick scrawls of an active young child pausing at her mother's side before returning to seek out brilliant red salamanders under rotted logs in the woods. The house was sold when I was sixteen, and we never returned. Not until my mother's 80th birthday, when she wanted to see it one more time, though I think with some trepidation; we didn't want our memories of it tainted—and they weren't. We drove down the same dirt road winding through trees. And the house was still the same barn red—nothing had changed. No large additions, beyond a small swing set.

When my mother spoke of her own childhood lake memories of Sunapee, most often it was to cite that summer when she was ten and her parents gave her that small tin of oil paints, along with the rowboat after Arthur died—the summer she first realized she wanted to be an artist. But if not back then, at least in retrospect, my mother recognized the paints and the rowboat for what they were, ways to keep her occupied while her mother was off playing golf and lunching over at the old Sunapee lodge, when she wasn't resting on her bed, succumbing to her grief. She would always say that my grandmother never got over the loss of that, her first born son.

Those Sunapee stories wouldn't come alive for me until I found those carefully typed letters to her father—some about her riding lessons, watching sailboat races, an evening spent with her mother "listening to music," or about going to New London where her mother bought her "the cutest little animals you ever saw, they have wooden bodies with paper legs and tails." But mostly about that longing. How she missed her father, most "dreadfully, most terribly, and it is getting absolutely too hard to bear."

"It is not very bad without anybody to play with at all but it is very very bad without you..."

"Oh! Daddy I miss you so badly that I really don't know what I am going to do. The only comfort is that when you come you will be able to stay for a long time."

The only time she seemed to spend with her mother was on those errands to New London, or at the Sunapee Lodge listening to music. Otherwise, when not practicing her riding for the horse show, young Betty, with the wild curls and small blue eyes, seemed left to her own devices: "It has been rather a dull afternoon. I do not know what Mommy and Roland and Jack have been doing this afternoon for I have been reading a book through." The "been reading" actually crossed out, changed to "I have read through."

She would write about whether or not she could see Mount Sunapee, and I imagine long moments of her gazing out that open window, across the lake. Much of her time clearly was whiled away in the actual typing of these letters, the only sound beyond the lake lapping against the shore, the staccato of the keys purposely hitting the paper: "Mother is up at the golf course playing golf and Jacky is out in his boat. Roland is fixing his boat and nobody home except me and the maids. I had to stay home because I had to wash by socks and rest for my horseback-riding lesson this afternoon. We miss you an awfully lot, especially me."

I can wonder now if this longing wasn't finally one sown by her mother's very absence. Whether the real longing was of a child not for her father—but for her mother.

It was when I had a family of my own that we returned to the idea of renting a house on a lake, and maybe a twist of fate that we wound up on Lake Sunapee, originally for a family reunion on my mother's side. Over the years, we rarely stayed in the same house twice, I think because nothing compared to the barn-red Vermont house so central to both our happiest recollections. We sought out the rustic of wood stoves and pine paneling, mismatched coffee mugs, and the simplicity of wicker chairs, but were disappointed by garish '70s blue-and-pink lamps, or the updated which we liked even less, of wide-screened TVs, granite counters and digital washers and dryers. We were disappointed we finally could not recreate a time in both our lives together we would have happily relived.

And each summer became more difficult for my mother. Derek was working and could only come up midweek, and so for several days, I was on my own with my mother and the boys. While I tried to find the most practical as well as charming rental, every year we would arrive to find I'd made a mistake; the renovated cottage with fancy doorknobs my mother had trouble opening; the high queen bed she had trouble getting out of.

Most of all, I tried to avoid houses with stairs, but one summer, I failed to account for stairs leading down from the dock into the lake. When it came time for my mother to get out of the water, there was no railing to support her up the steps. I offered her my arm but she decided instead to sit down, and bracing herself, nudge her bottom up each step.

The boys were still in the water. Lucas had monopolized the one blow-up dinghy. Owen had tried it once, futilely stabbing at the water with the two-ended paddle. "I'm scared," he'd announced, and that was the end of that. He was examining a very hairy "poisonous" caterpillar he'd spied along the grassy shore.

Now sitting on the dock, my mother couldn't get up—as frail as my mother could be, she was actually quite heavy. It was not as simple as my giving her a hand to pull her upright.

Her idea was to "scoot" in reverse on her bottom down the length of the dock, to where she could then leverage herself up another set of steps, three stone ones, up to the grassy embankment.

"Mom, you can't scoot."

"Oh, I do this all the time at home."

"*Mom.*"

She laughed at my astonishment. "My Dear. What do you think I do when you're not around? I manage. That's what I've always done, that's what I do."

This kind of comment put my teeth literally on edge. It was the same thing she'd said to me a few weeks earlier, when I was visiting and she'd fallen in her bedroom, while I was in the kitchen cleaning up. I came in to find her on the floor, in the same position she was now on the dock. "Don't help me," she'd said. "I have a system."

A system?

I learned that day that my mother's "system" was exactly this, to scoot on her butt—then, it was across her bedroom floor, over to her built-in bookshelf so that she could turn herself over onto her knees, and, leaning one hand on the shelf, push herself up so that she could sit on the chair. I imagined that was her plan now, for when she reached those stone steps, where there actually was a railing.

I had watched her then as I did now, deeply frustrated by what I had always admired about her, that stalwart independence. And embarrassed: drawing attention to herself in this way, in front of her own grandchildren. Lucas was paddling mindlessly, staring in a kind of horror at Gramma. Owen, forgetting about the caterpillar, retreated behind a rock under a big leafy tree where he stared unabashed.

"Mom, please. This is stupid."

"It's not stupid! I can do this!"

It takes a very long time for a very elderly lady to scoot on her bottom.

"Give me your hand," I demanded.

"No. Not yet."

I stood there, steaming in the sun. It was suddenly incredibly hot. In the heat, the entire lake seemed to go still.

What felt like hours later, she had made it to the end of the dock. Then turning over onto her knees, she leaned on the second stone step, trying to reach the railing—rickety as it was. "*Now* you can give me a hand..."

We argued—I couldn't just give her a hand. I needed to heave her up from behind. She argued back that she was too heavy. She insisted that I give a hand.

Owen came out from behind his rock. "Gramma?"

"Not *now* Owen!" My patience was gone. Evaporated into the steamy air.

"But Gramma?"

"Yes, Owen?" she said sweetly, as if he'd just asked her to look at his latest drawing of the adventures of "Mr. Fluffy."

"Gramma, a person can't *give* a hand. It would be all bloody. And they don't sell hands in stores."

My mother laughed. She was laughing so hard, she had to sit back down, so her legs now were sprawled out on the dock. I found myself laughing too but not at the joke. At my mother, sprawled on the dock, large and unwieldly, her pale veined legs cocked at odd angles like she was some enormous dropped doll. We laughed until our sides hurt, the way we always could laugh together, when we could forget what we were laughing about in the first place.

Owen looked hurt and annoyed. He retreated back behind his rock. "Just don't get *bitten*, Gramma, by that caterpillar. It could *kill* you."

This made her laugh even harder.

But the laughter softened her resolve enough so that she considered now my suggestion of lifting her up. "You won't be as heavy if you can scoot yourself up to that second step," I said.

Which she did so that she was then in a sitting position. So that I actually *could* "give" her a hand and heave her upright.

Another summer, I made an even worse mistake: I rented a house up a steep hill from the lake.

"Why on earth did you get house on a *hill?*" My mother

shrilled, as we were commencing the treacherous walk down it for a "dip," as my mother still could refer to a swim, which by now had become as much an expedition as shopping at CVS or her doctor appointments.

She tentatively navigated the uneven stone path with her cane. Her other arm was hooked firmly through mine.

I didn't bother to answer that I wasn't thinking *hills* that year, I was thinking a beach area where she could easily wade in and *out* of the water without having to scoot on her bottom down a dock.

Lucas was out in our rubber dingy thing again. Owen had tried it but was still too afraid. Now they were both in the shallow area, Owen whining because *whyyyy* couldn't Lucas go row out to pick one of the bright yellow water lilies to put in a bowl like we would every year? The lilies were just a stone's throw from the beach, but Lucas said no, he was "busy right now," what I would say to him when I'd be on the phone with my mother, helping her to open another chicken.

At first I thought he'd finally relented, and that it was Lucas in the rubber boat.

It was my six year old who was rightly afraid of going in over his head.

And without a life preserver.

Or a paddle.

"I'm *scared*!" Owen's voice echoed across the cove. Distant and mournful as a loon's.

"*Damn* it Owen!" I tried not to use that word around them. But my son was drifting away. He could drown. And my mother, leaning heavily, dependently, on me, could *fall*.

"Go," my mother said. "Never mind me—just get me to that tree."

A couple of steps ahead was a big sturdy pine, and she reached for it.

I stumbled down the hill and dove off the dock. An afternoon wind had whipped up the currents and he was quickly being carried out of the cove.

The current kept shifting so he was just out of reach.

"*Mommmmy! Mommmy!*"

An older man puttered by in a rowboat with an outboard motor. Swiftly sizing up the situation, he puttered over to Owen. He latched his own boat's rope to the dingy.

"What were you doing, little buddy?" I could hear him ask, as I swam toward the boat. When I reached them, out of breath, treading water beside the boat, he looked down at me. "Got to watch these currents."

I couldn't see his face against the glare of the sun, but I felt his scrutiny—I was a lapsed mother.

The man asked which was our house, and I pointed to the one up the hill.

He towed Owen while I hung on to the back of the dingy. Owen dragged one finger in the water, delighted now by the ride, which infuriated me.

I was relieved to see that my mother no longer was teetering by the tree, had made her way over to an Adirondack chair up the hill. She was a tiny speck, and I was grateful for that distance. It was a space I could call my own for a few brewing moments, where I was free to storm in silence. For those few moments, in that breadth between me and my mother, to revel in some fleeting freedom of not giving a damn at all.

Though anger still seethed beneath my increasingly thin surface.

Once we were on the beach and the man had puttered off, I took Owen by his shoulders and spit through clenched teeth, "What were you *thinking*?"

Owen looked astounded. He didn't seem to remember his own terror. There was only this, the now. How I was stamping out that sheer delight of his boat ride.

"Yeah, you didn't even have a life preserver on," piped up Lucas, wading watchfully in the shallow area.

"Shut up!" I snapped.

Now it was Lucas who looked astounded. He leaned down to cup water so that it ran out between his fingers.

Owen opened a tight fist. Crumpled in it was a water lily.

I let go of him. Remorse weighted me down as suddenly as a heavy rain.

Owen's face contorted. He began to cry silently. He started up the hill, letting the crumpled lily fall from his hand.

I went rigid. It was too late to undo what was done, and I had only to watch him stumble tearfully up the hill, on his little bow legs.

Then there was my mother's voice. "Owen, Look! Look at that *bird*!"

Even from that distance, she could sense our tension. As she had that afternoon when we were driving to her cardiologist, and she reminded me that this too would pass.

Owen didn't answer. My mother could guess at what had transpired without having witnessed it. Back at her house on Long Island, once when we were walking up the beach, she had seen me rage like this when Lucas ran up ahead, out of sight, with Owen loyally following behind him. She'd told me to never mind her then too; I'd left her teetering in the sand, to run after them, straining to see them against the blazing afternoon sun.

"Owen, come sit with Gramma so you can see."

He went and stood behind her chair until she patted her lap. He came around to sit with her.

"See that huge bird, right there? On that birch tree! Oh, I wish I had my bird book. Lucas, come see this *bird*!"

Lucas disconsolately made his way up the rocky hill. I followed behind, each step feeling harder than the one before.

We all peered at the birch tree.

"I think it's just part of the tree, Gramma," Lucas said.

"No, it's *not*." My mother insisted. In her ever-insistent way. "It's a *bird*. See the beak? Its head keeps moving!"

"Gramma, you're having a brain fart," Lucas said.

I gently smacked Lucas on the back of his head.

But I diagnosed the brain-fart as the double-vision she could complain about, which quite possibly might make a beak-like branch appear to be moving its "head."

I was weary. "It's a stump on the tree, Mom."

"It's not. Right there. It's a *bird*."

Lucas started back down the hill. "Well, let's see if we can make it fly away then."

"No, that's mean, don't startle it!" My mother yelled.

Lucas was already trail-blazing through the bushes.

Then he was climbing up the tree, until he had reached the "bird." Shaking the branch with the stump, he called out, "See, Gramma?"

My mother threw back her head then. She laughed. The way she had always laughed, a kind of silent exuberance that bubbled up deep from within her belly. The way she had laughed sprawled out on the dock, contagiously, so we were all then laughing.

Lucas came back up the hill.

And then the real moment: Lucas squeezed in beside Owen to sit in her lap. "I don't want to break your bones, Gramma. Let me know if I'm breaking you."

In my mother's last years, I learned to revel in moments of resurrected calm. Like the calm of the lake first thing in the morning. Before the wind whipped up those currents. When the only ripples might be cast by those delicate water bugs just skimming the glass surface. The "water spiders," what Owen called them, because they could walk on water, gave us hope in the miraculous. When my mother still had the strength to really swim, I remember how she used to do the breaststroke, that sharp angle of her elbows like wings. How she could never swim a straight line along the shore, and I'd wait for her to realize that she was curving out toward the middle of the lake, heading into the distance, or at the bay back on Long Island, out to sea. She no longer had the stamina to swim laps. But when not treading water, she could float on her back. "Oh, this is *heaven!*" she'd cry up, into the sky.

12

If there was a denouement to my mother's final years, it would follow the loss of her driver's license. "My life ended there," she would say, about no longer being able to drive even the one block radius to the post office and grocery store. It was all in the knowing. She needed to know that she still had that, the freedom, which she didn't, to get in her car and drive. This pivotal chapter begins when I drove the boys out to celebrate her 93rd birthday on September 9th, and her car was missing; it wasn't in the driveway.

Without her cane, she greeted us with open arms and wobbly hugs. As if her car missing wasn't perhaps news.

I had to ask: "Mom, where is your car?"

"I'd rather you ask me where my cane is—I can't find it."

"Here it is, Gramma," Lucas said, reaching just to his left, where it was leaning against the foyer wall.

"You know, you've always been such a good finder. Always finding my glasses."

He shrugged. "They're usually right *there...*"

I rested my hands perhaps a little too firmly on his shoulders; Gramma was forever flattering Lucas, as a way of forgiveness for the one time she mistakenly gave him a peanut butter cookie and he broke out into full-body hives.

"It's my birthday. I'll tell you my little saga later," my mother chirped, too happily.

"What does saga mean?" Owen was collecting new words like he did rocks.

Then I saw them: carpet swatches. My mother had been threatening to go carpet shopping ever since the cats peed on her bedroom one, when she'd been away with us on vacation at the lake. I took a deep breath, calculating these clues, realizing she'd driven all the way, three towns over, to the carpet warehouse. Far outside that one-block radius.

"Mom, where *is* your car?"

"It's my *birthday!*"

It *was* her birthday. And who knew how many more there would be, so I had to let the car subject rest, though my palms were sweating as when she would do this, keep things from me, increasingly, her falls, the reason she now kept a stepladder in her room for when she couldn't reach that bookcase.

Every year, the boys helped me plan a little birthday party for her, my tribute to her really, for all of my own elaborate birthday parties when I'd wake to the magical transformation of our dining-room table, replete with balloons, streamers, accordion paper centerpieces, and, back then, not goody bags, but carefully wrapped little gifts of pick-up sticks, or kaleidoscopes—we were a bunch of little girls, holding them up to the light, dazzled by the reflected brilliance of colored plastic beads. I'd carried on this birthday tradition with the boys, though pirate or Spider-Man-themed, with goody bags of plastic eyeballs and spiders.

This year, because she was a "girl," they'd insisted on a princess-themed tablecloth and bought her a child's plastic crown with pink rhinestone jewels. The crown was too small, but Gramma wore it anyway. It stuck up like some kind of satellite on her head. Lucas and Owen made huge cards that they folded into tiny squares and hid for a treasure hunt. They loved treasure hunts, and excitedly called out "hot" or "cold" as my mother poked around the room, lifting up seat cushions and the edge of couch throws with her cane.

She took a long time to unfold the cards, each with free-spirited drawings, and a scrawled "I love You". She was trying to stand up the enormous cards on the party table, when Lucas asked, "So, Gramma, where *is* your car anyway?"

She leaned toward him and whispered, "I hid it."

Lucas looked confused. Not believing this, but not quite entirely disbelieving, as was true with the Easter Bunny, Santa, and dragons. If he and Owen had been a few years younger, the prospect of a treasure hunt for a car might have sent them skipping outside, to seek out the car under Gramma's rhododendrons.

"How can you hide a *car*?" he asked.

"*Magic*," Gramma said.

"Magic?" Owen piped up. Owen loved magic. In the next couple of years, I'd wind up forking out hundreds for magic lessons at a local Halloween shop. "Gramma, watch this." He rubbed a balloon on his sweater, then stuck to his cheek.

"Oh, how do you *do* that?" Gramma exuded, clearly grateful for the distraction, grinning too broadly—she showed her perfect front teeth, a gorgeous bridge. In every photo I have of her, even from our wedding, her smiles are tight-lipped, to conceal her naturally crooked teeth. She'd finally invested in the bridge after a couple of her front teeth crumbled into bits. Owen knew about the crumbled teeth as he found them one day in the antique salt dish. He'd thought they were an artifact, old mouse bones, she'd dug up from her yard.

The smile lingered long enough for Owen to peer into her mouth, the balloon still stuck to his cheek. "Did you know Mommy's teeth are falling out just like yours,

Gramma?"

My mother looked at me.

"They're not falling out," I began dubiously. "They're just a little...loose...."

When I'd first announced to my family that my dentist said my wiggly teeth were a result of teeth clenching, they'd all looked at me as my mother did now.

"A whole *lot* of them are loose," Owen added gleefully. "Because she chewed right through her night thing that's supposed to keep them from falling out. Isn't one of them *this* one?" he proudly pointed to the space where one of his own front baby teeth had been extracted due to an infection.

Lucas looked stricken. "Are they really going to fall *out*?"

"They're not..." I was suddenly tired. "Yes, it *is* the two front teeth. And yes, they're wiggly. But they're not going to fall out." I hated when I was at a loss for words in front of my own children. "And Owen, it's called a night guard. So I won't clench. Which is what loosens teeth."

"You clench your teeth?" My mother was fully my mother in that moment. The concerned mother for her child. She was worrying as she had just that previous week when she was back in the hospital, and I had to drive home in the dark and torrential rain. Three years later, shortly before she died when again she had to sign the DNR: a nurse asked her what were her wishes, and she answered, "I wish for my daughter to be taken care of."

My mother carefully folded a piece of wrapping paper from the Sherpa Soft Surroundings cardigan I'd given her, along with sweatpants for her physical therapy sessions to help improve her balance. I used to buy her interesting sweaters and jewelry for her birthdays, when she still went places. Now what seemed more gift-worthy was the practical of sheer comfort.

She saved wrapping paper for future use, as she would rinse out and reuse freezer bags and aluminum foil, putting me to shame for throwing anything out. "You worry too much. You clench your teeth because you're always worrying. Stop worrying."

Stop worrying? *Your car is missing.* I thrust my tongue between my teeth so I wouldn't clench them.

I wasn't like my children, when it is normal to have wiggly front teeth. And I wasn't elderly like my mother whose teeth crumbled and fell out, the hard bits saved in that salt dish to show her dentist.

"Stress is most often a factor in clenching," my dentist told me. This was in March, when I went home to stress over my stress levels, to examine them up close as I do my children's splinters. Panic had gripped me as it could most days, when Owen poured his own juice from a freshly opened gallon jug into a tiny plastic cup, to flood the kitchen floor, or climbed on the counter to devour an entire bottle of Flintstone vitamins. The acute psoriasis I would develop on my scalp I would learn also was a stress "factor," though not until after my mother had been buried for two years, when it finally would clear up for good.

I tried to remember when I first started clenching my teeth. I couldn't remember. You *can't* remember. You only find out at your six-month checkup, when your dentist is able to wiggle your two front incisors, numbers eight and nine.

My dentist told me not to bite into bagels and to reduce my stress levels. *Stress.* The previous winter I'd spent driving back and forth to my mother's twice a week through blizzards, as she was recuperating from a fractured pelvis. I'd get home in time to pick up the boys from school, although once when I got home early enough for a short nap, I slept straight through their dismissal. It was a call from the school that woke me up, and I found them sitting stoically side by side in the principal's office, clearly appalled that their own mother seemingly had forgotten all about them. Then I'd take them home to concoct some tasteless pasta dinner; to insist on homework before I'd play audience to Owen's magic tricks of vanishing quarters; to pacify Lucas in his latest fixation, usually something he wanted but knew he couldn't have, like an iPad or a $200 life-size stuffed dragon. Before resorting to the diazepam, it was Benadryl, and after several glasses of wine, when my husband finally came home, I'd disappear upstairs to take two capsules so that I could drift off into a thick fog.

My mother finally told me about the car, after we'd had cupcakes, after the boys had gone outside to talk on the toy cell phones from their goody bags they'd picked out for themselves from Target's dollar bins. They were pacing my mother's deck as they'd seen me pace our kitchen, with my own phone cradled on my shoulder while trying to make another tasteless dinner and talk to my mother struggling with chickens or seltzer bottles. Lucas was stirring an invisible spoon in an invisible pot. Owen was opening and closing invisible refrigerator doors.

My mother and I were still sitting at the party table littered with cake crumbs, broken noise makers and spilled juice as if it had been a raucous party of ten rather than a mere two children.

She told me the "little saga" of how she was parking in the handicapped space outside the carpet warehouse, when she stepped on the gas pedal instead of the brake—and slammed into their front window.

"You crashed their *window*?" I pictured shattered glass, a shattered windshield, wondering how she'd escaped unscathed.

"Not the window exactly." She went on breezily to relay the details of it really being "just the brick wall" *beneath* the window.

And she still was able to come home with carpet swatches.

"Well, there was no sense in just standing around waiting for the police. I mean I'd driven all that way..."

This actually made sense to me, to us, and I'm sure only to us—not to the police who had to ferret her out amongst the stacks of carpet in the back of the warehouse. I knew that getting dressed, getting there, had been an ordeal. I knew how much it meant to get done what she needed to get done, despite having slammed her car into a wall. So yes. I could understand perfectly how she would walk away from the scene of an accident to go pick out carpet swatches.

"They're just too close together, those two pedals," she said.

"Mom, car pedals are like that. There's a good reason—so you can make a quick switch from the gas to the brake."

I expected her to counteract me. She didn't.

"They said I may have to take a driving test."

And then she told me about how her insurance didn't cover collision and it would cost $2000 out of pocket to fix the car. "I don't know if I should spend it."

The boys had abandoned their cell phones for the simpler pleasure of blowing bubbles, and blowing gently into the little plastic wands, they forgot they were children pretending to be adults.

Usually watching the boys would prompt comments about them, how different they were, how fast they were growing. About how my mother wished she could live long enough for that, to see how they both would "turn out." She didn't say anything. It unnerved me when my mother was at a loss for words; it didn't happen very often, hardly ever in fact, in her resolve to have things addressed as she saw fit, from how silverware should be loaded into the dishwasher to signing petition after petition to bring home our soldiers. Resolves I saw as too perfectionist, but others as huge-hearted, if not heroic.

"Mom, you have to get the car fixed..."

She spread out her arthritic fingers across the princess plastic tablecloth, as she sometimes did to examine their knobbiness, to remark on how she couldn't believe how old she was. "Not if I can't drive anymore."

13

My mother did get a new carpet installed in her bedroom, a blue to complement her paintings on the walls, all of grayish blue tones, the color of the beach in winter, except for the small one hanging in one corner that always reminded me of the sun in spring. And she did get her car repaired, if only because she couldn't show up to the driving test with a crushed radiator; the suspension of her license arrived in the mail, along with a Driver's Ed booklet and a date when my mother was expected to appear at the Department of Motor Vehicles. She had been issued a mandatory appointment for an "interview" and a road test. My mother carried that booklet around the house with her, in the wicker bag she kept on her walker, along with her sketchbook, pens and a prayer book that mostly went unread.

In preparation for this appointment, she also was issued a mandatory eye examination form to be filled out by her ophthalmologist. Dr. Ludlow was three towns over, and we barely made it in time, my mother, once again, not dressed when I arrived at the house.

By the time she settled into his chair, she was exhausted. "If you could just sign this..." she said, waving the DMV form at him.

Adjusting the large black goggle machine over her eyes, he explained about having to do a full examination before he could sign anything. Peering through his side of the goggles, he asked, "Ever see floaters?"

"I don't think so..."

"Flashing lights?"

"No..."

"Double vision?"

"Well, yes, sometimes."

"And when does that occur?" He asked.

"Oh, when I'm driving," my mother answered far too simply. "Sometimes I see two cars."

"Two cars?"

Two cars?

"In the oncoming traffic, to my left. But I quickly realize it's just one car." Then my mother realized what she had just dug—a deep hole, and so efficiently. "It doesn't happen much, just once or twice."

In the end, it didn't matter what she told the doctor. The double vision thing showed up in the exam. Several times in fact, when she saw double letters on the eye chart: two Ds. Two Ss. Yes, two Vs.

I was glad then that the doctor whisked in front of her face another eye-machine thing, so that we could not make eye contact. I was on this side of this latest digital apparatus, sitting in a chair against a wall. Seeing what he could see: An obscenely enlarged image of my own mother's eye.

He zoomed in closer. Her pupil morphed into a tar-black wobbly moon.

"Ahhh, you're still the queen of astigmatisms," he said, "But your lenses are beautiful."

"Well, thank you," my mother said. On the precipice of 94 "beautiful" took on a whole new meaning. "But my glasses are terrible," she went on. "Haven't been able to see with them at all—"

"Your prescription hasn't changed much," he interrupted blatantly. "It's macular degeneration."

For a moment, my mother and I slipped down into a mutual silence as we had when she was first diagnosed with breast cancer.

The screen went blank and my mother's monstrous eyeballs vanished. He moved the apparatus away from her face, explaining something technical, about the back of the eye, deterioration of the macula-something-or-other, but he was looking at me, so my mother snapped, "Talk to *me*. This is about *my* eyes."

Without missing a beat, he shot back, "I'm talking to you both."

"Well I can't *hear* you. I've gone a little deaf. Speak up."

"Your eye is like a camera," Dr. Ludlow roared. "Your lenses are fine. But the film in the camera is *shot*."

My mother blinked once. She folded her hands over her purse in her lap, settled her mouth into a thin hard line.

My mother who claimed she could see clearly, not only saw double, but evidently had one lens that was actually tilted, so that her eyes were straining to see in two different directions. And her "film was shot" so she might actually be going blind.

Her diagnosis was clear. She must wear glasses all the time, and even with glasses, she may barely meet the prerequisite for DMV.

"If they take away my license," my mother fumed, "I will go home and have a stroke!"

She stammered on about how she only goes up to the grocery store and to get her haircut. She only drives locally, except for that day when she went to the carpet store, and she only mistook the gas for the brake pedal because she was "flustered," having first missed the turn off to the parking lot.

Then Dr. Ludlow stood up, to stand over her. "I don't think you will go home and have a stroke just because you

maybe shouldn't be driving anymore."
My mother glared up at him. "You have *no* idea, do you. *None*."

I would take my mother to the retina specialist who thankfully confirmed that it was the "good" kind of degeneration, one so gradual, she would not go blind before she actually died. "Well, that's a huge relief," she said, "To know I'll only go blind once I'm dead."
I then took her shopping for a new pair of glasses, and in every optical shop, she left a pair of frames on hold while she moved on to the next shop, hoping for something she liked better. She left behind countless discarded frames strewn across every counter, and I was ready to like anything. *Any* pair. "These may be my last glasses. I want ones I *like*," she said, able to read all too well my impatience, so I roused myself from my frame-hunting stupor, and we moved on to the next optician. I mustered patience I really didn't have, even though I knew she was seeking something that didn't exist. The perfect pair.

My mother was to appear at the state DMV office of investigations on Tuesday March 24th. First floor. Window 22. Unlike for doctor appointments, we actually would arrive on time—my mother was up and dressed when I arrived to pick her up. She was sitting on the edge of her bed waiting for me, already in her coat with her hands folded over her purse. Breathing deeply, as calm as she could be when something was at stake. My mother could become hysterical when again she spilled her coffee "all over my brand new comforter!" But when it came to real crises, she could retain a calm as she did now.
Window 22 was at the far end of a long counter marked by 21 other windows—each window framed by ivy sprigs rooting in vases of pretty glass marbles. As if DMV could be any more inviting than a blood lab.

For the interrogation, a lady with a clipboard asked politely if I would "step away" from the window so she could interrogate my mother about what exactly happened when she drove her car into the wall of the carpet store. When she mistook the gas for the brake pedal.

I sat on a bench—just within earshot of my mother referring repeatedly to the brake as the "clutch." What she had learned to drive on, some 1930s automobile? I wanted to pinch her.

I could swear, above all the raucous of sorry waiting folk in this enormous DMV room, I could actually hear the mad scribbling of Clipboard Lady. "So you were driving a stick-shift then."

"What stick-shift? I was driving my car."

I took out my phone to play with it, when what I really wanted was a cigarette, though this was before I started smoking again, sneaking cigarettes out in any kind of weather on our front porch.

The lady beckoned to me, wearing the pleasant blank face of someone taking a fast-food window order. She told us she would meet us outside for the road test "and to take our time."

We had no choice but to take our time. My mother understandably was quite slow, and it had been enough to get her up the stately stone steps, through the metal detectors, to hobble down the long hallway. Now we got to do it all again in reverse. At least we got to climb down rather than up the stone steps....

Outside, Clipboard Lady was already there, leaning against the railing, feet crossed as if she'd been waiting hours. She wore her horribly pleasant smile as she told me to "find a comfortable spot to wait."

I sat on a "comfortable" stone step. Watching younger folks mostly, come and go, up and down the steps, as if back and forth to college classes. There were no other 90-

somethings in the mix.

They finally returned. Getting out of my mother's car, Clipboard Lady still wore a pleasant smile though it seemed to have stiffened a bit. "I'll meet you back at window 22. Do take your time."

My hobbling mother was giddy with relief: "I think I did pretty well." She'd been really worried about the parallel parking. She thought she'd aced that one, as "there were no cars in front or behind me."

We began our trek back up the stone steps, through the metal detectors and down the hall. To beautifully ivy-sprig-framed window 22.

It takes only 30 points to fail a road test. My mother failed by 95.

My mother stood at the DMV counter as Clipboard Lady went over all the points: making a 3-point turn in an intersection; almost hitting the car behind her parallel parking—

"What car? There was no car..."

Ms. Clipboard pinched two fingers together: "You missed it by this much."

She had failed to yield at a yield sign. "What yield sign?" My mother asked.

"You did a three-point turn in the middle of an intersection."

"What's that, I don't even know what a three-point turn is."

"A U-Turn. You did a U in the middle of an intersection." Then Ms. Clipboard suddenly became real. She put a hand to her heart and in the most gentle of tones said, "Mam, I was queasy out there..."

And I saw it: Clipboard Lady had feared for her own life with my mother behind the wheel.

My mother was quiet a moment. Then she began drawing a little map on the cream-colored counter with an arthritic pointer finger. The map of that one-block radius of her house, the post office and grocery store. "I don't go far. But I need to go up this block, turn right, then a left here to get my mail and groceries."

Ms. Clipboard actually grew patient, folding her hands on the counter.

We both looked at the invisible map on the counter.

Then Clipboard Lady just shook her head. "I'm sorry."

My mother leaned across the counter, her brass pendant swinging wildly. "You wait until you're 93." She leaned into Ms. Clipboard's face. "You just *wait*."

Ms. Clipboard "evolutioned" as my seven-year-old would say, back into an ice monster that he could "bust open" with a hammer. She handed my mother a copy of her failed report. At the bottom was scrawled the word "hazardous."

She slid another form across the counter for my mother to sign—for her to surrender her license.

And as my mother slid her license across the counter, I regretted this. I regretted it so deeply, I could taste the remorse, my mouth filling with saliva and my eyes welling. I regretted not having just taken away her keys, something I'd dreading having to do, but perhaps far less devastating than having someone take away your license—I hadn't foreseen Clipboard Lady actually asking my mother to surrender that little card she'd been carrying around her entire adult life. That identity. And dignity.

Outside, the sun felt too bright. We stood on the expansive stone steps of the DMV. Climbing those massive stone steps had been an ordeal, as she had weakened and her balance was precarious. And now, as I was navigating her back down them, she was unravelling: "They don't understand. I won't go far. I just need to go the store. When I run out of milk. Eggs. What do I do then? What am I going to do?"

She gave in to the unravelling, and we stopped on a

stone step. She leaned into the metal railing and began to really cry. "I'm a nonperson. I'm a hollowed-out piece of wood. I'm not a person anymore."

I held onto her, my hand wrapping around her thin upper arm, holding on as people passed us on those massive steps, swirled around us like a current. I held on to her to keep us both from being swept away.

14

I drove my mother home in her car she would never drive again. The van would sit in her driveway for another full year. "I should sell it," my mother would lament, peering out at it through her blinds, where it seemed crouched and resigned, wet leaves plastered to the windshield or snow alternately melting on its roof only to ice again. Her reasoning for not selling it was that the house would look vacant without a car in the driveway, and neither did I encourage her to sell it. In fact, weekly I would go out to start it up, to keep the battery charged, even as the tires slowly lost air. I liked those moments sitting alone in her car, the engine idling. A welcomed escape from my mother's small crises that seemed only to be mounting—estimated tax bills going unpaid, the skylight in her studio leaking. Although ironically, in that old van, I was escaping into everything that was my mother; I would root through her compartments, finding old winter gloves, hairbrushes, empty Tic Tac boxes, things I'd handle reverently. As much as I wanted to escape her, I wanted to surround myself with her in the small space of that car. Missing her as I could, before she was even gone.

The truth was, that beat-up old van was a comforting

constant in our ever-changing landscape of those final three years of her life, as much as it also was a reminder of the loss of her independence: "Do you have any *idea*? What it's like to be imprisoned in your own home?" she could rage on the phone, just as I walked in the door after visiting her, because we'd forgotten to buy eggs. How "ridiculous" it was that she couldn't just drive up to the store herself, and I'd worry that she would have, except that I'd never returned to her the keys once I'd driven her home from the DMV.

Having no eggs in the house was sure to enrage my mother. I worried she would have a real heart attack or finally, that dreaded stroke. My mother had been eating the same breakfast for eons, of oatmeal, an English muffin, and that single soft-boiled egg. She didn't want to feel even more dependent on me than she already was, by having to wait until I was able to drive out there again to buy her a dozen eggs. So when we'd forget something at the store, or even once when she needed a ride home from emergency because I had to return home to one of my boys who was sick, she'd call Regina.

Regina had been cleaning my mother's house ever since she first emigrated from Columbia, back when my parents first moved out to Long Island full-time. At the core of their relationship was an enduring devotion, one based on an equal admiration, respect, and real love; my mother watched Regina's children grow up and hung their drawings on her fridge. She listened while Regina cried when she found out her niece was having an affair with her husband. After my mother's falls, Regina sometimes spent the night when she first got out of the hospital, leaving for work after making my mother's breakfast, knowing to perfectly time her eggs, even to add just a smidgen of margarine to her English muffins. Regina would make her meals to freeze, and on her grave would leave a stone saying how much she missed bringing my mother soups.

Increasingly however, there were times when Regina couldn't drop everything to buy a carton of eggs, and so my mother would resort to finding her own help, answering ads in the local paper, and periodically placing her own ads. This always left me on edge, and when I'd plead with her to allow me to "screen" the applicants, my mother unfailingly countered with the fact that she was "perfectly capable" of hiring her own help. And so commenced a parade of aides—rather, a motley patchwork of relatively lost souls, really just decent and lonely folk: the wealthy middle-aged diamond-earring-studded woman with two terriers, seeking self-fulfillment by volunteering her time to the elderly; the retired agency aide with a wandering eye, who made the mistake of thinking my mother would enjoy playing Scrabble; the former manager of an athletic shoe store, who had found her "true calling" as a certified home health aide, and would strum James Taylor on an out-of-tune guitar for her clients. All souls who didn't last very long, as my mother's initial intrigue or compassion would wear thin when they proved incapable of cleaning out the kitty litter pan or taking the garbage out to the bins.

The only person who lasted for a relatively protracted period time, was Cassy, who drove a pickup truck, packed with tools, shovels, rakes and even an old mower. My mother would tell me about that too, how resourceful she was, even mowing lawns to pick up extra cash. I don't remember exactly how my mother found Cassy, but I remember her the best because my mother liked her the most. On our daily phone calls, my mother told me Cassy stories that would make her laugh all over again, like the time Cassy scooped up her neighbor's dog shit from her lawn, to fling back at their windows. She would tell me about Cassy's latest "outrageous" colorful outfits, and her "terrible" ex-husband who was defunct on child payments, and how "well-behaved and smart," her four-year-old daughter was when she'd have to bring her along, if she came after her daycare hours. Whose drawings, as well, wound up hanging on the refrigerator.

Unlike the other well-meaning but evanescent souls who dissipated before I had a chance to meet them, Cassy stayed long enough for us to have an occasional conversation out of my mother's earshot—my mother hated nothing more than if she caught me in "cahoots."

One time, Cassy waited until I was leaving, and came out to lean in my car window. She was wearing large plastic pink hoop earrings, and I could just hear my mother exuding over these "outrageous" ornaments.

"Listen, I'm not supposed to tell you. But you should know. Your mother sometimes has falls."

I must have feigned surprise at this news, that was not news.

In the middle of the night, Cassy evidently had come all the way from Montauk to help her up off the bedroom floor. "I don't mind really. I just worry about her, you know?"

I nodded. And in that moment of silence, I suppressed my resentment of her seeming to be telling me what to do. What exactly *was* I supposed to do, with such a head-strong mother? One who very well might love Cassy one moment and fire her the next.

"You know, I really like your mom. She's a real pip." Then Cassy said, "But she made me promise not to tell you. If she knew, she would *kill* me."

This was the part that *was* news to me: my mother keeping secrets from her daughter. Though I wasn't sure why. Was she really worried I'd put her in a home? Probably not. She just knew her daughter too well. She knew I'd be *mad*. Even though I might not know why I was mad. Though that was maybe the part she understood best: my own frustration. Because it mirrored her own.

I wouldn't tell my mother what I now knew but had long

suspected, that she was having these secret falls, ones when she no longer was able to get herself up by leaning on the stepladder or her bookshelf, until Cassy quit. Actually, Cassy quit a few times, since my 94-year-old-"pip"-of-a-mom wanted to retain control. Cassy also liked to be in control and could not restrain herself from organizing my mother's cluttered bureau into neat piles. My mother liked her cluttered bureau, so they would have spats, and one day the spat went too far. My mother accused Cassy of "throwing away" her money when Cassy splurged on a ball of fresh mozzarella cheese at the market that she didn't ask for. Cassy walked out without even serving my mother her morning's soft-boiled egg, telling her and she could go clean out her own litter box.

I was in my car when the text came: "I quit!"

I panicked as I could when one more aide evaporated into the ether, but truth is, I understood; I knew her feeling, of just wanting to walk away. From it all. From the fragile elderly mother who could vent, her only way of freeing herself mentally and physically from her entrapment, unable to drive, whiling away days obsessing over regrets and picking through endless catalogues.

I did receive a follow-up text from Cassy saying that she hadn't *really* quit, my mother just had pissed her off, and she never would do that, just abandon my mother. Cassy inevitably did leave, but only because she'd been offered a well-paying managerial job, and my mother was genuinely happy for her. And before leaving, Cassy secured her best friend who would now be the one to come in twice a day, between her waitressing shifts. But the best-friend-waitress wouldn't last long, as she made "tasteless" meals she served lukewarm, and "depressed" my mother with her unruly hair and drab sweatpants: "Who goes around looking like they just crawled out of bed?"

When my mother called to tell me she'd fired her, I was furious. "*Mom!*"

"It's my life, Sandy, not yours!"

Right, Mom, but now there is no one to get your breakfast, clean up the mess you leave in the kitchen, and mop up your spilled coffee.

So we were back to catch-as-catch-can well-intentioned folk who came and went, who briefly entranced my mother with their colorful pasts; stories of delinquent husbands who pawned their wife's jewelry or estranged children who only called to ask for money. And when the well-intentioned proved utterly ineffective—when I was finally the one to drag back overflowing wastebaskets to my own garbage pails and clean out the litter box—I resorted to a list of non-agency aides I discovered beneath piles of catalogues and charitable solicitations, probably from hospital discharge papers that she routinely tucked away.

Problem was, the list was so old, the aides were in need of aides themselves, if not already dead. Only one called me back. At nine o'clock at night. From the beach—she was fishing. She was at the lighthouse beach out on Montauk Point, actually standing out on those slippery rocks. "It's a full moon, best time," she explained, when the fish were "really jumping." The moonlit-jumping fish was all lovely imagery, but I was sick to death of the finding-the-perfect-aide quandary, so I interrupted her to ask about her availability.

Presently, she was employed only on weekend nights, to change diapers for an Alzheimer's patient. She was available days. Perfect.

When I called my mother to tell her I'd scheduled to have her meet this woman, she was furious. "You had no right to take that list. Stop taking my *things*."

"You need real help, Mom."

"I'm not bed-bound. I don't need an *aide*."

I assured her she wasn't from an agency.

"And I'm the one paying for it—I will find my own help!"

"Cassy told me." I sat down at my kitchen table as if

settling in for a rough landing. "About having to come over in the middle of the night."

There was a silence so pronounced, it sizzled across the distance between us. I could imagine my mother's mouth settling into that hard line.

"You weren't supposed to know about that."

"She was worried about you."

"Don't tell me I can't take care of myself. I've been taking care of myself since I was eighteen! And I took care of my parents when Daddy lost it all in the Depression. We were broke and I took care of them! You wait until *you're* 94, you'll see what it's like!"

I wanted to scream back at her, *I'll never make it to 94, never mind 54, the way I feel now, old and creaky and angry myself! That every emergency-room doctor, social worker and even your physical therapist has confirmed, in no uncertain terms, that you need more help!*

Instead, I was manipulative: "I think you'll like her. She fishes."

My mother laughed then. "She what?"

"When I called her. She was fishing."

My mother laughed and laughed. "Wonderful. A Fisherwoman."

We planned for the fisherwoman to meet my mother the next day, and I drove out after dropping off the boys. My biggest worry was that she would show up in those drab gray or blue aide outfits my mother hated. Said-fishing aide appeared next day, thankfully, in bright colors—bright pink scarf, turquoise earrings. Fuchsia pants, albeit, a bit too tight considering her enormous bulk.

She explained about her weekend routine of caring for her Alzheimer's client: she'd stop in for "seven minutes" of diaper changing before heading out to fish. Then she returned around midnight, still in her waders, and as not to wake the rest of the household, she used her fishing headlamp. This fishing aide had a huge heart; I could tell. She also had four cocker spaniels who had shredded all her rugs, but she didn't care about "such things"; nine siblings, herself the eighth; a wasp's nest just like the one she'd spotted in a corner of my mother's window: "Just mix liquid dish detergent with an ounce of water and pour it over the bugger."

I wasn't about to tackle a wasp nest with detergent. And huge hearts can be challenged by huge talkers; and this huge-hearted fishing aide wouldn't shut up. I watched as my mother's initial amusement began to wane. She was glassy-eyed.

The fishing aide caught me glancing at my watch, and I caught her crestfallen look. I realized, underneath the bright fuchsia-and-teal facade, underneath all the laughter, she was lonely. That perhaps she only had this night job because no one wanted to be awake around her cavernous laughter and chatter.

The cold hard truth was, I had to face up to my mother's own loneliness, and that was enough hurt in my own life.

15

Needless to say, we didn't hire the fisherwoman, though she probably would have been the most competent of the entire aide patchwork. And when all else failed–which it now had—we circled back to Regina and her own recommendations, however ultimately unreliable: her own mother who couldn't understand a word of English. Otherwise, my mother only had Geb, another sorry soul my mother felt sorry for, whom she hired to weed until she realized he didn't know a weed from a perennial, and fired him after he'd pulled up her entire garden.

At the time of my mother's most serious fall in those last years, when she almost bled out, it was another of Regina's references who was coming in daily to get my mother's breakfast, Susan, a young 20-something mother whose toddler's drawings as well, would wind up on refrigerator.

One morning, after getting my mother's breakfast before leaving for her day job stacking shelves at the local IGA, Susan laid out my mother's clothes carefully where she could reach them, and parked the walker next to her bed. But my mother, instead of using her walker, tried to stand up and balance on one leg to put her pants on. We'd been over this, how sitting was safest when getting dressed. But either my mother didn't remember, or she didn't have the patience she needed with her own limitations. Or both.

When my mother fell, she gashed her head on the corner of an open bureau drawer. She was on Coumadin by then, to prevent blood clots, and thus her blood was thinned to the consistency of tap water. Within minutes she gushed enough blood to saturate her new blue bedroom carpet.

This time, she'd activated her medical-alert button, and I got the call from the medical-alert folk as I was driving to Target.

A sugary-voiced girl informed me that an ambulance was on its way and asked if I would "be able to respond."

I was thinking errands. Target returns and the flash-drive I had to buy Lucas for school. I mumbled, "Well, I have to figure out my kids, who's going to pick them up..."

"But can you respond?"

I realized I was thinking out loud to someone who was just doing her damn job. Or possibly was just plain disgusted with my indecisiveness, as if I actually *wouldn't* respond—when your own 94-year-old mother is on route in an ambulance for literally the countless time, of *course* you respond.

So I did what I do when, once again, my mother was being whisked back to the emergency room as I had the previous week when she fell in the bathroom (Coumadin is also infamous for quite remarkable bruising). I texted babysitters who are never available when I need them, and I finally fell back on my last resort, to call Derek and ask him to leave work early.

This time, I found my mother not in a dim sea-foam cubicle, but in the trauma room, her face translucent under harrowing overhead lights. Her hair and knobby arthritic hands were encrusted with dried blood. She'd been stripped of her bloodied clothes, but under the thin hospital gown, I saw she was still in her underwear. Blood-soaked. I let escape a howl: "Mom! What *happened*?"

She shielded her eyes with a crusty hand against the glare of the lights. "I don't know, I fell..."

The nurse returned the bloody medical-alert button to me in a specimen jar. "She's going to be ok," she soothed, and I felt myself again the panicked child.

They hadn't allowed me in until after they'd stitched up her head, just before wheeling her down for a CT scan to check for brain bleeds. Then x-rays of her pelvis, hips and chest for fractures.

"Oh, *look* at me!" She gazed at her tremoring blood-encrusted hands, turning them over and over. "I don't understand...where am I hurt?"

"Your head, Mom. They stitched up the back of your head..."

"I don't remember what happened, only this sharp pain..."

"When you hit the bureau..."

"Is that what I hit?"

"You fell mom."

"I know I fell," she said. "You think I *want* to fall?"

There were all kinds of things I could have said then. About how she should be using the walker, that she shouldn't rely on walls, shouldn't try to balance on one leg for Christ's sake! She wouldn't have so many falls, if she wasn't so insistent on doing things her own way, rarely listening to the advice of anyone but always ready to give advice herself—especially to me.

The good news from the CT scan: no brain bleeds. Bad news, some fluid in the brain. Good news about the fluid in the brain was that it was some kind of normal elderly-brain fluid thing. Bad news was that she had a pelvic fracture. Good news was it was non-surgical fracture that would heal on its own.

And then I realized my mother was going to be ok—and tried to ignore that familiar nagging annoyance at this fact, like something stuck in my shoe. A nagging little uncomfortable pebble boring into my heel. It's a hard feeling to feel, that annoyance at the fact that the mother, whom you love deeply, actually will go on living. Wants to go on living. "I want to live to a 100!" she could pronounce, when doctors asked her age, or out of nowhere, pumping a weak fist up into the air. Because you can't imagine how *you* will survive if she actually *does* make it to a hundred.

To get my mind off that "pebble," I focused on attending to my mother by cleaning the blood dried around her fingernails with alcohol wipes, on shifting from the annoyed daughter to caregiver of an elderly woman helpless on a trauma-room stretcher.

And then another shift—as my mother started talking gibberish. Pointing across the brilliantly-lit room at invisible empty boxes that needed to be packed with napkins because the stove was on fire and we needed to fill socks with sticks.

And then she was mumbling something about *me*, in the third person. There was something she needed me to do but I wasn't here....

I leaned into her face. "Where am I?"

Even as she seemed unseeing, she must have seen my fright and said reassuringly, "You're right here, Honey Bun."

She nodded off, to wake again and mumble something about her brother, or an uncle....

I leaned in closer to hear. "Mom, what?"

"Oh never mind. Just pack up the boxes but do catch them first. They have holes in their bottoms."

"Mom..." it was the sound of my own voice but sounded distant, an evening breeze across the lake....

The now frightened adult only-child was running down hospital halls calling out "Something's happening to my *mom!*"

I found her doctor. He heard the fear in the frightened child and picked up his own pace back to the trauma room.

He asked my mother where she was. She said she was back on Staten Island—where we were not, of course, but where I grew up.

He asked if she knew who he was and she told him no, but he was very handsome.

He asked her to squeeze his hands and she could. And to move her toes and she could. And then she nodded off.

The test results showed no stroke. No brain hemorrhage. The "confusion" was a result of the concussion which, in older people, evidently can manifest more dramatically, but she was to be admitted for observation overnight. And then the doctor was talking to me alone out in the hall. I knew what he was going to say before he said it: my mother no longer could go on living alone. Before my mother was discharged, I would have to resort to what we'd always tried to avoid, full-time home-care. The ground seemed to shift beneath me. Two years later, I would be sifting through her ashes at my dining-room table, seeking the last of her, tiny whole bones. I would look back on this moment for what it was: the final descent in our trajectory.

Once admitted, my mother would wake up lucid, and rightly annoyed by her perfectly coiffed roommate who was threatening to have her own reflection in the window arrested, along with all the "bitch" nurses. The woman became unruly, tried to pulled out her own IV lines, and my mother demanded she be moved to another room. "Just because I'm old, doesn't mean I'm batty," she said.

The irony of that statement wouldn't be lost on me when months later, it would be my mother talking to her reflection in a hospital window. But back in that trauma room, as I'd listened to my mother mumbling like a truly old person, the frightened child felt abandoned. Because even at 95, my mother could still reassure me about my own mothering: "You're doing a *wonderful* job with those boys," she would state firmly, when I might express my doubts, my regrets about losing patience, about somehow not emulating my own image of the perfect mother.

"*Look* at a them," she'd said just last week, when I'd brought the boys for a visit. They'd been tossing a football around outside her sunroom window. The wind was blowing, whipping up their hair. "They're beautiful."

And the frightened 50-year-old child waited, watching as her mother slept with her head crooked at an odd angle, her pillow stained with dried blood from her encrusted hair. Waiting for her mother to return to her.

PART II

1

Chandice came "highly recommended" as do most aides from home-care agencies, as well as the only one available for long-term care on such short notice. She arrived late the night my mother was discharged, from the Bronx by bus, with a single over-sized suitcase, and my first glimpse of this tall, robust woman was of her large silhouette against the streetlight.

On the way home, she asked me to tell her about my mother. I don't remember what I started to say, only that she interrupted me with "No, *tell* me. What is your mother *like*?" I wouldn't realize until later that Chandice was less interested in getting to know my mother than preparing for what lay ahead. In the same way as she prepared by removing all my mother's kitchen knives from their holders, and requested I put away "any silver candlesticks," predicting that my mother might accuse her of stealing.

I don't remember what I answered, if I answered at all, as the drive from the bus stop back to my mother's house was less than five minutes. What I remember best was the bulk of this woman filling my car, in her heavy winter coat with a faux fur trim, and the glint of the street lamps off her large owl glasses; when I first brought her into my mother's room, how she stood at the end of my mother's bed, apologizing for the way she looked—when the agency called her, she'd hardly had time to pack. She pulled off a purple winter cap, combed her fingers through her afro. "Just look at my hair!"

Not having ever set eyes on this woman, we didn't know what her hair was supposed to look like, and for a moment my mother and I just stared at her—registering what suddenly was a fact: this woman, a stranger in my mother's house, had not come to visit. She had come to stay. I came and sat beside my mother, while Chandice stood there in her enormous coat. She rested her hands on the bed's baseboard as if standing at a pulpit. Neither my mother nor I had the presence of mind to suggest she take her coat off—I did not offer to hang it in the foyer. We'd both lost our voices as you do when caught up short, suddenly peering over the edge of a precipice. My mother and I would never be in the same way again.

Chandice moved in as she clearly had moved into many homes, remaking her bed with her own flannel sheets, a green and red plaid, what must have been some Christmas present. She kept a well-worn Bible beside her bed, and at times I caught glimpses of the heavily underlined pages, as Chandice stood before it, her hands raised in supplication. She would stay in my mother's house until the morning when she climbed the stairs to tell me that my mother was gone.

What I remember best about that first night in my mother's house, was Chandice's dismay. In the living room, she stopped short in front of my mother's old box TV. "What *is* this?"

I felt the weight of the question, as I had when she asked me about my mother.

"It's a television."

She gave me a deep frown I would come to know all too well, that would never fail to make me feel foolish and naive.

I explained that the only flat screen TV was the small one in my mother's bedroom. I had not foreseen the amount of time Chandice would actually spend in front of the box TV, how the hours would bleed into endless days holed up in the house without a car, with her laptop set up on an old trunk which was the coffee table, drinking her smoothie concoctions of kale, and green apple the color of pond scum. How long the days could become for someone cooped up 24 hours with a 95-year-old woman, with little reprieve beyond my twice weekly visits when I'd drive her up to the store for things she needed for herself, iced tea, almond milk, more kale and apples.

When I showed her the kitchen, I'm not sure what she expected, though I would come to assume she had worked for families of quite some financial wealth, with larger kitchens, big flat screen TVs, as well as silver candlesticks. I had yet to look at my mother's accounts, to actually calculate what Chandice was going to cost. Though I can imagine if my mother had been the one to calculate, she would have fired her before she'd taken off her coat.

She removed the knives and placed them on top of the refrigerator. And in response to my baffled look, she frowned again. But with some compassion said, "I'm sorry. But things can happen. Things I realize, you would not imagine."

From the spice rack on the wall, she opened a jar of thyme and sniffed. My mother's spices were so old, the labels had entirely faded.

She held up a jar to my nose. "Smell that?"

I didn't smell anything.

"Exactly."

My face flushed with an embarrassment that surprised me. Maybe because the spices had gone untouched for so long, the rack was coated in a thick film of sticky dust. Truthfully, my mother hadn't really cooked in years, beyond the salmon steaks I used to pick up for her, or eye of the rounds she'd grill up with onions.

Chandice asked would I please buy all new spices, including ones my mother never owned, cayenne pepper, caraway, and ground mace. She then sniffed my mother's sponges, replaced them gingerly on the sink. She asked me please to buy her dish rags she could sterilize on the stove.

"And where's the blender?"

At the time, I didn't know my mother even owned a blender, though Chandice would find it stored behind truly old baking pans. Her eyes grew wide with dismay. "How can she not have a blender?"

I showed her the Cuisinart. She frowned. "We will need a blender."

I was tired of feeling embarrassed and foolish. Then I remembered the baby monitor I'd picked up from the local K-Mart, only because the agency had suggested it. A *baby* monitor for my *mother*. I hadn't been able to bring myself to open it.

Chandice did so now, taking it out and setting it up on the butcher's block. "You've done well, girl."

I was ridiculously pleased.

We returned to my mother's bedroom, where my mother was getting out of bed.

Chandice went to help her, and my mother shooed her away. "Please. Whatever you do, don't hover."

Chandice took a step back, though not before placing the walker in front of my mother. She stayed close behind as my mother started her laborious trek to the bathroom.

When Chandice started to follow her into the bathroom, my mother turned to shut the door. "I would like my privacy, please."

Chandice and I stood outside the bathroom.

"She will be ok," I said.

Chandice only frowned.

Then she asked "Are the gloves in there?"
"Gloves?"
"Disposable."
Now it was my turn to be dismayed. "What do you need *gloves* for?"
"My Dear. I will need gloves."

After I left, Chandice would text me other things we needed: shampoo, body oil, Preparation H, alcohol rubs, lightbulbs, new batteries for chirping fire alarms, potting soil (her plants were wilting), calcium supplements. Weekly now she'd text me a list for Peapod delivery, but we could forget staples she would run out of like olive oil and pepper. Soon after she arrived however, my mother developed a fever and was readmitted to the hospital for a kidney infection.

The morning after she was discharged, Chandice called me first thing in the morning, while I was driving the boys to school. I had just pulled into the school parking lot when she called to ask me this: "Have you *seen* your mother's *vagina*?"

This question, a proclamation really, was loudly emblazoned via Bluetooth–the mother of all microphones–in my Odyssey minivan.

Both boys went dead silent in the backseat.

Lucas abandoned his frantic search for a baby tooth which had, quite literally, just fallen out in the backseat. "Gramma's *what*?"

Owen, at the buck-toothed-silly but mature-beyond-his-years age of eight, asked point-blank: "What's wrong with Gramma's vagina? Is it okay?"

Luckily, Lucas *did* find his tooth, miraculously amongst the bits of gravel from their boots. He was anxious to get into the building now, to head to the nurse's office to retrieve a cool plastic tooth necklace which later he would come home parading.

I sat in my dirty momma minivan until the boys had disappeared safely inside the school, trying to decide whether this question about their Gramma's—my *mother's*—vagina was a rhetorical question or a query that actually needed answering.

The previous week when my mother was in the hospital, I'd glimpsed her vagina more times than I cared to count; when she hadn't been sitting on bedpans, nurses were whipping out wet chuxs from beneath her sore bottom. But no, I hadn't seen up *that* close, to perceive that it was "red and swollen," as Chandice went on to describe, as I was pulling out of the school parking lot, turning onto main street, forgetting where I was going.

Chandice went on to make tskking sounds of great disapproval: "They let them *sit* too long," she said, meaning the truth about incontinent hospital patients. Chandice was convinced she'd contracted the infection while in the hospital from her last fall.

She asked me to pick up Vagisil, along with Calmoseptine, her most trusted barrier cream, one she had sworn by with all of her past demented incontinent patients.

"And *please*...get the Depends."

Chandice had been trying to get me to buy Depends since she first told me I needed to buy gloves: "We will need them sooner or later, and I'd rather have them...sooner." But I no more wanted to roam the incontinence aisle than later I would home-care stores for special mattress pads for her bedsores, and the correct bandages for her gangrenous leg. And on my first foray down the "Incontinence" aisle, I was not fooled by the genteel commercial packaging of uproariously happy aged ladies sipping coffee on pristine white couches. Because I knew *that*: There was no way in fiery hell, my mother, even in *any* kind of demented stated, would agree to wearing what she would know very well was essentially, yes, a *diaper*. And I knew about diapers, though the assortment or brands for preemies, newborns, toddlers, pre-toddlers, was equally mind-boggling. It's one thing to figure out your baby's size —but your *mother's*?

And then what style? Well that *depends*. On whether you plan on wearing a Depends beneath a pencil skirt—then you might need to slink into the Depends "Silhouette Briefs." Then there's Depends "adjustable underwear," for the woman on the go...If you need extra *extra* Depend protection, there's "Protection with tabs" Depends (with a wetness indicator! Extra leakage protection! Six-tabs for "discreet open changing!" As if "discreet" and "open" aren't *oxymorons*....)

I could not bring myself to buy anything more than what appeared to be an oversized maxi-pad—which Chandice unwrapped to unfurl in front of me: "This is *not* Depends."

Since that original Depends conversation and then this big "V" one, Chandice and I had already had several discussions about my mother's bodily functions. I was not entirely uncomfortable with these discussions, well familiarized with them from my children's own share of diaper rashes, bouts of constipation and accidents. It was all part of motherhood. Now it was part of daughterhood.

But Depends. *Diapers*. For my *mom*.

When did she become *this* dependent?

I couldn't bring myself to buy the Depends until my mother finally had a real accident, a bowel movement all over her bathroom floor. One night, Chandice called and minced no words in letting me know the mess she had to clean up.

I was flipping burgers for dinner. I had to feed my family while discussing feces, the phone cradled on my shoulder. I apologized to her for having to go through that, and Chandice was point-blank: "Dear girl. I would rather clean up *shit* than stick my fingers where they don't belong." She went on to discuss—in detail—constipation, and to tell me about having to put her finger up "clients'" butts when not even enemas did the trick. And before hanging up pleaded, "But please. Do please pick up a package of Depends."

Now my mother officially had had a real accident and I had no choice. The Depends choice which most closely mimics real underwear seemed to be the "Fit-Flex." When next I drove out, Chandice examined the bulky Depends package and gave me one of her sage nods. "You've done well, my girl."

"You'll never get my mother to wear those."

She smiled broadly. "Oh, no?"

It was the first time I noticed what a large gap she had between her two front teeth.

She beckoned me with one broad index finger to follow her into my mother's room.

My mother was lying on her bed.

Except for the occasional trek to the sunroom my mother stayed in bed because she no longer felt like she was living in her own home. "This isn't my house anymore," she would complain to me on our daily phone calls. She'd complain about the stranger, dressed in her aqua-aide uniform, who cooked her own recipes of fried shrimp and stews with my mother's pots and pans. Who whipped up her own healthy concoctions of kale green apples and ginger in that old blender she finally found.

Chandice opened a pair of the Depends to display for my mother. "Mrs. Tyler! Look at *theeeese*! Aren't they pretty?"

My mother did look at them. "What is that?" She asked flatly.

"Panties. But pretty and lacy. Wouldn't you like to try them on?"

My mother took them. "Well, they are pretty..." she

said, dubiously.

Pretty? "Pretty" was a word my mother hated, especially when someone used it to describe her paintings. It implied saccharin and precious which her work was indeed not.

Besides. My mother was never a pretty-lacy underwear type. More a practical *Fruit of the Loom* underwear wearer. But she agreed to try on the lacy Depends. Which frankly still stuns me.

Though no more stunning than when Chandice called to tell me about my mother being up nights, getting dressed to go out at 3 am—then locking her door and refusing to come out.

2

It was a Saturday morning when Chandice called to tell me that my mother had been up all night, changing clothes, trying to decide what to wear. I imagined my mother laying out different amalgams she'd wear to art openings, pairing them with her printed scarves or pendants.

When Chandice reminded her that it was only 3 am, my mother screamed, "So what if it's 3 am, I can still go out!" Then she'd locked herself in her room because people were plotting to kill her.

And supposedly, Chandice was in on the "plot," with me.

It was not even Chandice's plot. It was *mine*.

I must have gone silent, because Chandice said, "It's not about you. It's her mind."

Her mind.

"But you need to come out here now. And take the lock off that door."

This time driving out, I should have been preoccupied with scenarios of what could happen in the time my mother was locked alone in her room: a particularly dangerous choice, as her balance had become so precarious, I could envision her falling, to hit her head again on the corner of that bureau. Instead, I was preoccupied with what was new, this paranoia. My mother's short-term memory was deteriorating, and I wasn't surprised by her wondering at the stitches in her head, feeling for them as if something were caught in her hair. And even the paranoia wasn't entirely new, my mother convinced it was "kids making mayhem" with a pack or cards found strewn across the coffee table (most likely the cats' mayhem), or someone had stolen a new shower curtain she remembered buying, that had "vanished," (I would find it buried beneath a pile of clothes after she died, when I was cleaning out her closet). What was new was this paranoia about her "good daughter." About me.

Chandice greeted me at the door, in a pair of moccasin slippers. As if she lived there. Which she did. Entering my mother's house now I could feel like a guest in my own home.

She was looking quite put-together in her bright aqua aide uniform, but her owl-shaped glasses could not hide the shadows under her eyes; she had been up every night with my mother for a couple of weeks by then, sometimes until 7 am. And she did not drink coffee or tea. Nothing caffeinated. Only Silk Almond milk. Grape juice.

She told me my mother locked the door after Chandice tried to pick up my mother's clothes strewn across the floor, knowing she could easily have tripped and fallen over them. It evidently wasn't just nights when my mother was rooting through her closet; she could change her clothes several times a day, and whereas she used to be vigilant about hanging up her own clothes, adjusting her blazers just right on their hangers, now she left a trail of discarded shirts and pants across her bedroom floor.

"Please," Chandice said, leading me to my mother's bedroom as if I didn't know my way. "*Talk* to your mother."

I called to my mother through her door, and at the sound of my voice she opened it.

"Sandy! Oh, it's so good to see you!" she exclaimed, as if I never came to visit, as if I hadn't just been there that week.

My anxiety turned swiftly to anger, in stark contrast to my mother whose face brightened at the sight of my own.

"Mom, you cannot lock yourself in your room."

"Oh, did *she* tell you that?" she hissed.

Chandice had been hovering in the hallway, and with an exhausted frown, she now retreated into the kitchen.

"Well, it's none of her business," my mother said. 'Because it's not *your* business." She shook a fist in the air. "Oh, she drives me crazy, following me everywhere, even to the bathroom...I can't even get dressed without her hovering! I like my privacy, is that so terrible?"

"It was 3 am, Mom! What are you doing up at 3 am?"

"It was? Well, I couldn't understand that, why it was dark out," she said and we both laughed.

We both still could laugh.

My mother sat down heavily on the edge of her bed. "She even goes through my drawers."

"Why would she go through your drawers, Mom?" When what I really wanted to ask was *How could you think I was plotting to kill you, Mom?*

"Things disappear."

"Things disappeared before Chandice came."

"You don't understand what they do. This is my house! They act as if it's not my house!"

The "they" was her aide, and when I reminded her that there was only one person, my mother countered "Well, she *feels* like many people," the way "they're" constantly traipsing back and forth through her room, to get to the laundry room. "And she's just wearing out my machines!" She was on the edge of tears. "I know my mind isn't quite right. But this isn't right either. You have to talk to her.

But be on my side, please. Not theirs. Mine. I need you on my side!"

There was nothing like the "taking sides" argument that could set me to clenching my teeth so that my whole jaw ached, and for a moment I remembered what I had forgotten, that I was overdue for the dentist, as well as any other of my own doctor appointments.

"Well, you don't. Why is that. You never take my side? Even when they took away my license. That's where my life ended. That day."

Of all the things my mother could forget, she had never forgotten that moment when she'd slid her card across the DMV counter. Just as she had then, she now drew the same little map on her bed. "All I need is to go up to the store one block and back. I was fine on my own as long as I could just get my own groceries." She looked at me. "You never spoke up for me then either."

There were all kinds of things I could have said then. *So it was my fault that you lost her license? Was I the one who rammed my car into the wall of a carpet store? And if you hadn't locked yourself in your room, we wouldn't be having this age-old argument in the first place.* We could have snapped and screeched at each other as in the past, I could have remained as obstinate as I had at Ikea about not wanting a new couch.

Instead, I sat down carefully in the fragile rocker. I stared at the new blue carpet already stained from so many spilled coffee mugs. There was just the slightest change in hue from where her blood had pooled when she'd gashed her head. I marveled at how Regina had been able to clean up a rug saturated with blood.

"You have no idea what goes on," she said. "You're not here. So you have none. *No* idea."

The fragile rocker creaked beneath me, and I felt then the tremendous weight of it all. How this finally was true. I really didn't know what went on when I wasn't there. It was my gut as much as my head I now had to rely on for guidance in my choices about my mother, besides reassurance from my therapist about my making the right choices. Still, I felt on the verge of tears as I could waking up mornings now to my mother's pleading phone calls for me to fire this woman. About how she couldn't stand another minute of having someone in her house "every second." That is, when she could remember my phone number at all, which increasingly she could not even where I had written it on the bottom of that ceramic tile she'd use as a coaster on her bedside table. She would have to ask Chandice to dial it for her.

My mother was now pounding her bed. "You have to believe me, Sandy! The things she does! She even drank all my Scotch."

"Your *Scotch*?"

"I asked for a light drink and she claimed not to know where the Scotch was." Then she looked at me. "Please, Sandy. Just *talk* to her."

I would have liked to have my own tantrum. To pound my own fist into her bed: *What the hell makes you think she'd want to drink your Scotch? And stop telling me what to do!* I would have liked to slam my door on her as I could when I was a tween. I couldn't have a tantrum because I had to quell my elderly hysterical mother's hissy fit as I only had to otherwise, with my kids. But, although I wasn't at all sure what I was supposed to talk to Chandice about, I promised her I would.

Chandice was in the kitchen. We stood across from each other at my mother's butcher's block table. "Dear girl," Chandice said, her eyes swimming behind those huge glasses. "You need to believe I don't go through her drawers. Your mother asked me to open a drawer for some socks and that's how she remembers it."

I looked down at the cracks in the worn table. *That is*

how she remembers it would be a phrase repeated many times over the course of the next 18 months.

"And I don't even know where she keeps her liquor. The reason I couldn't make her a drink."

I realized then that Chandice had overheard our entire conversation on the baby monitor in my mother's room; she had the receiving end set up now on the butcher's block.

"Even if I did know, I wouldn't drink the stuff," Chandice said. "I don't drink. It makes my knees weak."

"Your knees?"

Then Chandice and I were laughing. Giggling really, on the edge of hysteria. But in our laughter I felt a betrayal of my mother—her aloneness back in her bedroom surrounded me now like a cold chill. I felt quite suddenly, despairingly, sad. It came over me like a flu, and for a moment I wondered if I wasn't actually sick.

Chandice must have sensed this, because then she said, "You know, this can make you crazy."

She told me about a client's daughter who wound up in a psychiatric ward because she couldn't accept the "truth" about her mother. Rather, a truth about what her mother had become—one Chandice already understood I would not be able to accept about my own mother.

She reached one large hand across the table to put it over mine. "Oh, my dear girl. You have to understand something. This is all new to you."

I could have countered with the fact that this wasn't entirely "new." I could have told her about my father, his own forays in the middle of the night. How I'd witnessed his own mind go too, although over the course of many years. I didn't because otherwise this *was* new to me. Because now it was my mother who was slipping away— receding into that deepening night, leaving me to cry out for her across the lake.

I removed the locks, not only from her bedroom door, but her bathroom one, as she was known to lock herself in there too, and one morning, my mother called: "You need to put the locks back on the doors. When are you going to do that?"

Why did she always have to call when I was trying to get the boys off to school? Older now, they were able to button their own pants, but distractions still reined and undoubtedly we were late getting out the door for one reason or another.

I was surprised she'd remembered my phone number—or maybe she'd just remembered where I'd written it down on that tile next to her bed.

Initially she called to tell me this: "I've been waiting here all night for my dinner and I'm hungry."

It's breakfast time, Mom.

"But it's so dark out."

I thought about explaining about daylight's savings. I didn't.

"Well then what time is it?"

"Seven, Mom. In the morning."

"Oh, I *am* losing my mind."

You're not losing your mind, I said tepidly.

"I just wish everyone would stop treating me like I'm an imbecile."

"Who's treating you like an imbecile?"

"Oh, everyone. Everyone just assumes I've lost it. They come and go back and forth through my room, wearing out my machines, but they can't even bring me my dinner!"

My hands began to tingle, and I took a deep breath; no time to spiral into a panic attack just as I was trying to propel the boys off into their day. The breathing made me suddenly tired, and for a moment, I was overcome with an exhaustion that could come over me now.

"And we need to talk about this. Why you would do such a thing."

Do what, Mom?

"Take the locks off all the doors. Why would you *do* such a thing? It's not just my door. You've taken the locks off all the doors in the house, so anyone can come in and murder me."

Murder.

Mom, why would I do that? Take all your locks off?

"Because you think I'm losing my mind and might wander off."

"If I thought you would wander off, wouldn't I be sure the doors were actually *locked*?"

I was relieved when she laughed, although I wasn't sure whether she was laughing because she finally did see this as nonsensical, or because she could not make any sense out of it at all.

Either way, thankfully we were able to move on to more sensical things; she asked me about the boys, and I told her about how Lucas refused to help me clean his frog's tank; how Owen left his dirty underwear lying all over the house; and, sorry, I was going to have to get off the phone, as the boys would be late for school.

"Ok, I will let you go," my mother said. "But I just need to know: are you trying to put me away?"

I stood stock still in the middle of the kitchen. "What?"

Why are you thinking that? Why do you think we've hired a full-time aide? So you can stay at home.

"I feel as if all communication between us has broken down," she said. "Between you and me."

I stared at a Lego left in the middle of the floor, and I was grateful for that. The expected.

"You could have told me you were going to do that," she said slowly, steadily. "You could have talked to me about it."

"Would you have let me take the locks off if I had?"

She didn't say anything. She was so quiet, for a moment I just listened to the static of our landlines, that distance

crackling between us.
"You're not my daughter anymore."
She hung up.

3

You're *not my daughter anymore.*

When I talked to my mother an hour later, she was enjoying a "delicious" chicken noodle soup Chandice had made, and I was already her daughter again. She asked me to buy birdseed for the chickadees "flocking" to the feeder, having forgotten what I really thought she couldn't have, how our communication had, indeed, "completely broken down." After she'd hung up on me, I stayed rooted where I stood, staring at that Lego, stunned that this other life of mine continued on around me, with Legos where they were left, and then a popsicle stick stuck to the rug, a squeaky squirrel dog toy under the table. Even before her mind started to go, it wasn't so unusual for my mother to hang up on me, when we might not talk for days. And in the hanging up, yes, we might feel the distance. But we never truly felt disconnected. I didn't feel as I did now—alone in a way I never had before. Not in this life, the only one I'd ever known, lived so closely alongside my mother.

In *Circling my Mother*, Mary Gordon's own mother's slow disaster was spread out over a period of eleven years, until her mother was reduced to a mental shell, her cheeks permanently bruised from pressing her face into her hands all day. Before my mother's concussion from this last fall, she showed only signs of short-term memory loss. But since having a live-in aide infringing on her space, the memory lapses seemed to have become more acute, and she virtually had no short-term memory at all. When she called now, conversations were boundless, circling back around to the same topic from two minutes previous, about how the tree outside her window had sprouted "enormous" branches in just the space of a day. If I dared to counter that trees cannot spontaneously "sprout" entire branches, she would insist that the green was "closing in" around her. I would change the topic to the safest, the weather, or whether or not she needed more birdseed.

On bad days, even safe-weather topics could be imperiled by the imaginary, as when she imagined she was left sitting in a dental chair or locked in a dark cold church. I say bad days because these hallucinations in addition to the paranoia were a new dimension to her dementia, to this slow disaster. A dimension I would come to find particularly heart-wrenching to navigate. Besides hearing lawn mowers in the middle of the night, she'd hear people making a "raucous" in her foyer, moving her flowerpots around outside her bedroom door. She could understand these for what they were, hallucinations: "I know there's no one there. But I still hear them." I could be talking to her on the phone, and she would call out, "Oh, what *are* you all *doing* out there?" Neither of us seemed able to accept this: my mother's mind actually going. Shrinking in on itself, like the sea sponges that washed up at the bay and hardened in the sun.

Chandice would warn again and again about how this could make me "crazy," telling me those stories of distraught, deranged daughters across my mother's worn butcher's block table—in what would come to feel like Chandice's kitchen, with her own large looming red Kitchen Aide, and her bake pans piled on top of the refrigerator she'd lugged in suitcases from her Bronx apartment. She would try to teach me how to navigate the "disease," the onslaught of paranoia about not only my plotting to kill my mother, but about my father being kidnapped. She would teach me the hard lesson of not talking sense to my mother in these moments, only to promise her I would go find my father and bring him home. Promise to stop them from torturing her with andirons up her rectum. Promise as you would not just a frightened but a truly panicked child, that you would make everything all right. But at the time, I wasn't really listening; while I respected Chandice, I didn't much like as tolerate her, because somehow I already knew that only Chandice by herself would be able to heave my mother into the wheelchair and on and off the toilet; to support my mother on her side while managing with one hand to change the dressing on her bedsores. I knew she would be the only one, quite literally, capable of fulfilling that unspoken promise to my mother about dying in her own home.

My mother continued to be up nights, and I called Dr. Craig to prescribe some kind of sleeping pill; she coolly informed me that any additional medication for a 95-year-old might only worsen her disorientation. She might even still be experiencing the effects of the morphine administered in the emergency room from her fall, even though that was now weeks ago. I talked to her about the "slow disaster" seeming to have become accelerated, and her response was that maybe not—maybe it only seemed that way to me, because, before now there was no one there 24/7 to observe her. But I could no more hear what Dr. Craig was trying to say than I could Chandice about the "disease." Because I was remembering another time when my mother was disoriented, when she'd had a urinary tract infection, the last one leaving her to imagine there was a third cat in the house. After all, UTIs can affect you mentally, as far north in your body as south. There *could* be a *reasonable* explanation.

Whether or not to humor me, Dr. Craig agreed to the UTI test. So the next day, after getting the boys off to school, I drove to Amagansett, stopping at the doctor's office for the specimen cup and wipes.

"Whatever gives you peace, Dear," Chandice said, snapping on her disposable gloves, and I resented that she too seemed to be humoring me.

But my mother wanted her "privacy."

"I can do it myself," she said, clomping her walker into the bathroom.

Chandice shook her head at me.

With the door open a crack, I was able to spy on my mother in her bathroom mirror. I watched her try to sit, then stand with the cup between her legs. She began to totter as if about to fall, and I burst into the bathroom.

"Oh, give me my *privacy!*"

"Mom, you have to let someone help you."

My mother lowered herself back onto the commode over the toilet, gripping the handles as if planning to stand again. "I can do this!"

And there we were, in a brand-new unchartered territory: my mother sitting on the toilet, me holding her by her shoulders as she looked up at me. "No," I said. "You. *Can't.*"

Her mouth settled into that hard thin line. "Get out."

"*Mom.*"

"I can take care of myself. I've been taking care—"

"You're not eighteen anymore! And you can't even remember yesterday!" Out of sheer desperation, I told her the truth. That her mind wasn't working right. That she could not even remember all the times she has been in the emergency room from falls, but I remembered them too well. That she could not even remember how she had gotten the stitches in her head, and she reached up now to touch her head. "What stitches?"

"You *fell*. You almost bled out. You could have died."

"Oh..." She was fingering her scalp, straining to remember.

"Mom. You have to help me. Because, I don't know. Otherwise...I am going to be sick."

And as I said that I felt chilled by a new fear—one for myself.

She looked up at me then, not angry. But worried. About me. She was my mom again.

Another wave of exhaustion came over me as it could most days now, and when I least expected it. I wanted to lean my head on her shoulder, and for a moment I did. I burrowed my face into that soft pink Sherpa sweater she always wore, what I wouldn't realize smelled of her until after she died, when I'd ball it up to muffle my wailing.

She reached up to pat my head, worriedly. "Oh, Honey Bun. I'll do whatever you need me to do." She handed me the jar.

4

The UTI came back vaguely positive, most likely from a contaminated sample, as I wasn't wearing gloves when I'd knelt between my mother's legs after helping her pull down her pretty lacy Depends—when she went all over my hands, and I told myself *this too shall pass*.

Dr. Craig prescribed antibiotics anyway, as she too was trying to give me peace—what I *did* finally need so that I *wouldn't* be sick. But I can't say even now whether I ever found peace. One as elusive as the little child in a blue sweater later my mother would see at random floating in the air; she'd gesture at it rapturously as she used to at the rare monarch butterfly that "came out of nowhere" to flutter past us on our beach walks.

But I do remember clearly the night I finally stopped trying to reason with my mother; the night she called to tell me that my father had been kidnapped.

My father who had been gone by then 21 years.

Where was I for *this* phone call? I don't remember. What I do remember, is my mother breathless with panic: "Sandy. They've taken him. Your father."

This particular call from my mother radiated such anxiety, for a split second I believed my father was still alive, snatched by a couple of hoodlums from the guest room where he used to sit at an old card table for countless hours bent over a jigsaw puzzle.

"Daddy?"

"You have to find him."

"Mom..." *Oh my god, Mom, really?* I wanted to laugh the way you do when something both awful and ridiculous happens, like dropping your car keys down a drain pipe stepping out of your car.

"No one kidnapped Daddy."

"*Sandy.* You have to find David!" She screeched. "You have to find your father!"

My mother's voice shook with a real fear. A terror so palpable, for a teeny tiny instant, I felt the same fear for my father's safety, imagining him, however unfazed, being driven away in some clandestine car while gazing out the black privacy window at the lovely scenery.

"Sandy, you never believe me. But *believe* me, I don't know what's going to happen...you have to go find him..."

To break the too real reality of this dream-like state, I fell back on what I needed: to *know*.

So I asked: "Who?"

"What?"

"Who kidnapped Daddy?"

"It was *them*."

I thought back to where we lived on Todt Hill on Staten Island. Over the years, the mafia bulldozed old neighborhood houses to build palaces with gilded front doors, fountains, and electronic gates, and we only came to know our neighbors as that, the shady "them." Paul Castellano, the boss of the Gambino family lived two houses up from us on Benedict Road and was shot and killed just two weeks after we drove away behind our moving van. If we'd still been living there, we might have made it on the nightly local news, the road I grew up cordoned off by police tape.

"They were looking in the windows." *Who, Big Paulie? The Howard Hughes of the Mob?*

How could this *not* be funny?

Because it finally wasn't. Because my mother was genuinely terrified.

And it was night. I knew how she could see her own reflection in the windows.

"Are your blinds up, Mom?"

"Sandy, please!" she screamed.

I remember where I went then. I went into a dark room, my husband's office. I didn't shut the door. I sat at his desk, in just the light from the hall. He still had his big old Mac monitor then, even though he worked now on a laptop. I sat in front of its black screen.

"Ok."

"You will? Go now?" She was trying to catch her breath, and my job then was only one: to calm her down. To eradicate the terror.

"Yes. I'm going to go right now."

She started to cry. "Oh, thank you. He must be so scared. Please. Call me when you find him." She was crying. Her voice shook.

"I will. I'll bring him home, Mom..."

I will never forget the relief in her voice. "You will? Now?"

"I'm going now. I promise. He's ok."

"Ok...Please, Sandy..."

"Mom, it's all right. I'm going now."

"Yes, please. Call me when you find him."

"I will. I promise."

I sat there with the cord phone to my ear long after she'd hung up—maybe even for real, hitting the "Off" button. I stared into my husband's darkened computer screen. At my own thin reflection.

Finding peace would be my coming to terms with the

inevitable only months later, on what I knew would be her last birthday. She would turn 96, and I would ask my nieces and nephew and all my mother's cousins, to send flowers. By transforming her house into a vibrant albeit overwhelming garden, I was making peace with the hard fact that she would not live to see her next birthday. The gangrene had not yet set in, nor had she been stricken with the stroke. But by then, she essentially would be bedridden except for when Chandice moved her to a large recliner, the only place she found relief from the bedsores on her tail bone. My mother was so inundated with glorious bouquets, she grew restive and Chandice had to remove the vases from her room.

5

The first time the boys met Chandice was when she made us Thanksgiving dinner, a couple of weeks after she arrived. "Oh, let me *cook*!" she'd pleaded, with an exuberance I didn't have the heart to challenge. Most Thanksgivings it was just us, and we'd opt to go out to dinner. Otherwise, it would have been me slaving alone in the kitchen for hours, with my mother trying to help by taking far too long to peel potatoes, just so we could all scarf down an over-or-underdone turkey in two minutes, before the boys scrambled off their chairs because they didn't like turkey, anyway.

Besides, I did not love to *cook*. Not as Chandice clearly did, now with a collection of spices much larger than my mother's had ever been.

But this year, I wasn't thinking turkey. I was thinking about the fact that this would be the first time the boys were visiting with this stranger now living in their Gramma's house. It made me deeply uncomfortable, and I didn't know how to talk to them about it. Maybe I would just continue to keep up a front for my mother's sake; she did not want to seem "old and decrepit" in front of her grandchildren. And when they were really little, there was no need to keep up a front—visiting Gramma was to be surrounded by her aura, to be buoyed along by her spirited ways; she was always eager to see them and most animated. Equally eager, the boys would scramble up her steps into the house as they would out onto the playground. You could count on Gramma for her own treasure hunts: "You're getting hot, noooo cooold..." She'd tuck away carefully-wrapped little gifts in her shoe boxes, and the boys would tear into them, to pull out bubbles, bouncy balls, silly squishy creatures, leaving her shoes scattered across her closet floor. In summer, we'd pack up our beach gear to go to the bay, my mother's high-back beach chair with the attached canopy, and they'd race back and forth from the water to show Gramma the minnows they caught in the colorful plastic pails she bought them every year from the local hardware store. They'd sit at her feet while digging deep holes with their new shovels. She'd walk up the beach with them, and with her cane, point out shells and desiccated crabs for them to collect. Out on the deck, she even managed to play games of kick-the-beach-ball without falling over. Back in her studio, she'd pull out those old collage materials so they could glue their own messy collages, of seaweed and other beach detritus, scraps of plastic mesh, bottle caps. She was fond of creative messes, and with their finger or poster paints, she encouraged them to paint broadly, sweepingly: "Fill the *whole page!*" She gave them hammers (until I replaced those with little kid hammers) to pound nails into scraps of wood from old painting stretchers. Lucas was fascinated by the large contraption she used to miter the corners of her stretchers, and liked nothing better than to root around in her tool box, to play with her wide assortment of wrenches and pliers.

Back then, the boys would sleep the whole drive out to my mother's, waking rested and ready for Gramma adventures. But having outgrown naps, Gramma visits had become more problematic, starting with that drive: "Why is it always so looong?" One or the other would whine, and I'd wonder about my decision not to buy a DVD player for the car, a lame attempt at trying to reduce screen time. Instead, I'd give them each a pile of picture books to thumb through, or their Etch A Sketches. I'd play one of their music CDs, and if I was lucky, they'd grow quiet, gazing dreamily out their windows. Lucas might lose himself in his own world of "action spider," where he made his hand crawl up and down the window. If I got really lucky, they might tell me things otherwise I would miss in-between hustling them to and from school, especially on those harried days when I was going to and from my mother's, like the time when Owen was six and he told me why you should never smile at a monkey: because he will think you are baring your teeth for a fight. "And don't *ever* touch an electric caterpillar because its spikes will kill you." Lucas once told us all about how humans don't believe dragons actually existed only because no evidence has been found: "they came before the dinosaurs. So far back, the bones crumbled away. That's why there are no fossils." He often would remind me not to step on the tail of his own invisible dragons, and sometimes on these rides, a smaller pet dragon would be riding on his shoulder like a parrot.

Now, once we arrived at my mother's, that aura seemed to have dissipated. As hard as my mother would try to muster up the animated, visits felt deflated. Since losing her license, she couldn't surprise the boys with little gifts, and would insist on my picking something up for them, though bouncy balls and bubbles no long went as far as they used to, not since the introduction of Iron Man and Pokemon cards. They'd quickly grow restless, wandering the house, as I didn't like them playing outside because of ticks in the badly neglected backyard. Owen would want to play with the fireplace andiron, dangerously wielding it like a sword, and Gramma thankfully would suggest, "Let's all go to the *park*!"

I didn't even know there was this public park until my mother suggested it. She must have heard about it from Regina—maybe her own sons used to play basketball over there, even though they were now grown. The park clearly had been around a long time, with weathered basketball nets and even more worn tennis-court nets. But for free, you could borrow dead tennis rackets, as well as dead balls, and that was enough to please the boys. The first time we went, they were thrilled to just grab up a bunch of the tennis balls and swat them around, careful not to hit Gramma who was working on her posture, trying to stand up straighter while exercising on her walker around the court's perimeters. Other times, they might shoot dead basketballs while my mother and I walked around the little track which actually had been repaved, unless little kids were riding their tricycles and I worried they might catch a wheel on her walker.

But my mother could tire quickly and we'd go back to sit in my car, especially when the boys were riding their scooters on the skateboard ramps. While they started by borrowing the park's rusted scooters, I wound up buying them new ones plus the full gear, of helmets, elbow and knee pads, so they would actually look forward to coming again.

Back in my minivan, my mother and I could just see their heads rise and fall above the rim of the ramp, and my stomach would clench every time they disappeared back down.

"Oh, I wish I wasn't such a bore," my mother could say, sitting beside me, pulling at some tissue balled in her lap. Somehow the tissues wound up dropped all over my car, and I could cuss them along with the boys dropped Goldfish.

"You're not a bore," I would say. Maybe too tepidly,

because she could shoot back, "Well, I know I'm not. But I am so *sick* of my *body!*"

I don't know if I ever responded to that, as it was something she said often. And as she was daily living out this frustration, spirited but trapped in the weakening of the physical, what could I say to make a difference? *That she would be feeling better soon?*

I never did talk to the Lucas and Owen about the fact that Gramma was deteriorating. Nor did I probably need to. We can forget how easily children can figure stuff out on their own, and I'm sure they figured out that their Gramma was in need of help, from her having been clomping around on a walker for some time now. Never mind the odd elevated seat thing over her toilet. One or the other might fish out her Sock Aide Easy gadget from under the bed (great for racing matchbox cars), and help operate the claw on her "Grabber" to reach under her bureau where a bottle of pills may have rolled.

The closest we ever came to actually talking about the reality of Gramma's situation perhaps was once when Lucas brought it up, when he first figured out what exactly a graveyard was. We were in the car again, passing the one behind a Catholic Church we always drove by on the way to the grocery store. We'd passed it countless times, as it was on the way to just about everywhere, Stop & Shop, Carvel, the post office, their pediatrician. Yet, neither boy had ever before remarked on the funny oblong stone things sticking out of the earth.

"Mom, what *are* those stones, anyway?" Lucas asked.

We were at a red light. I was not surprised by big questions, which always seemed to come up in the car. Like the time I had to explain to them exactly how boys differ from girls "down there," after they saw their first naked girl toddler, at a friend's house. Though I had a feeling

Lucas was old enough to already know about graveyards; maybe he just needed now to ask the question.

"Are there dead people there?"

"Yes, Hon," I answered perhaps a little too off-handedly.

"So...there are bodies there? Under the stones?"

Seemed like a very long red light. "Yes, Hon..."

"Is Gramma going to be in a place like that one day? Under a...stone?"

I hadn't yet reserved the columbarium niche at her Church. I didn't know how to tell Lucas his Gramma would be reduced to ash. I didn't know how to bridge this conversation at all.

"Gramma is really old," I said.

"I *know* she's *old*..."

"Everyone dies, Lucas," his little brother piped up. "But then you just come back to life again. And that just keeps going on forever..."

I was speechless. And that's fine, since they seemed to be working out this issue between them. Giving me a minute's space to figure out how my six year old had been able to come to his own conclusion about death. Maybe Sunday school way paying off after all.

But then Owen said something else, this time under his breath.

I asked him to repeat it.

"And when you're six, your parents can go away, too. Right?"

I had to look at him then, in the rearview mirror.

"That's right. They can die too." Could I dare to follow up with *but nothing is going to happen to Daddy and me?* Could I take this moment that far just for the sake of a quick comfortable closure?

My sweet boys were looking at me far more questioningly about this truth than the ones about gravestones or anatomical differences, and I had to look away. I couldn't have been more grateful for when we pulled into the parking

lot at Stop & Shop.
"But you know what is even worse?" Owen then said.
Lucas and I both looked at him. We both wanted a good answer.
"Having two heads."

On Thanksgiving, Chandice had been up since dawn to get the turkey in the oven before my mother woke, finding the old roasting pan covered in cobwebs in a cabinet, along with her Pyrex pie plates. She'd even pulled out the large blue carving plate and amber glasses that I remembered from my mother's own Thanksgivings; unlike me, my mother had been a master at entertaining. She'd decorate the table with paper turkeys, elaborate arrangements of colorful gourds and napkins, golden candlesticks. She'd bring out the best silver, family silver that went back generations, that she passed on to me when I married, which has long since tarnished in some corner of my attic. My half-sister's whole family would come over, and Catharine and my mother would have pie-baking "contests" to see who could make the best pumpkin or pecan pie. My youngest niece and I would steal the paper turkeys to play with behind the big drapes in the living room after dinner.

It was shocking at first, to see these things surface from my childhood, things I'd forgotten: the elaborate scene of a windmill and river on the platter. The intricate design etched into the rim of those amber glasses. As shocking and disorienting as having someone else moving around my mother's kitchen as easily as if it were her own.

I think the boys were perhaps a little shocked too, not so much by the incredible food spread but by how Chandice greeted them—exuberantly, leaning down into their small faces with those big glasses, clasping her hands between her knees as if resisting wrapping them in a bear hug. When dinner was ready, she ushered us to the table covered with one of my mother's good tablecloths, and I wondered if she'd dug it out from trunks herself or if my mother actually had remembered where she kept it. My contribution was a single paper turkey that wouldn't stay upright. I didn't think to buy two, but the boys weren't interested in it, anyway. Thanksgiving was probably Lucas's least favorite holiday, especially one prepared at his Grandmother's house where he had his first and only severe food allergic reaction.

I don't know what I expected and clearly neither did my mother, whispering to me, "Is she actually going to eat with us?" While I certainly didn't expect Chandice to take some small helping for herself to eat alone at the kitchen table or in her room, neither could I imagine us all sitting down together. So far, I was most concerned with just keeping Chandice happy—as if I was the one working for *her*—which mostly meant buying the correct brand of strawberries and silk milk, but also doing as I was told in crises like taking locks off doors. I knew little else about her. Sitting around my mother's table, I couldn't imagine us having a conversation any less stilted than one amongst estranged relatives forced to break bread together every holiday. I sat across from Chandice, next to my mother, feeling as diminished as my mother looked, hunched over her plate.

I need not have worried. Chandice held us enraptured, talking easily about her dreams of opening her own bakery and maybe selling cakes online, even having gone to baking school, and about her daughter back in Jamaica who was a kindergarten teacher, whom I already knew about; weekly, Chandice instructed me to wire a certain amount of her pay to daughter via Western Union. So weekly, I stood at the little red phone at our local CVS, reaching out to a place entirely other than here, a world away from my privileged one. I'd push the little buttons that would stick, stabbing at them, hoping for a connection, that at best was staticky.

Sometimes the phone was out of order, and I'd worry about what it meant if her daughter didn't get that money. Other than that, I didn't think too much about this daughter; I didn't want to start liking Chandice. Not the way I would wind up laughing with her in the kitchen, my mother alone in her room, bewildered, angry, lonely.

But at that Thanksgiving dinner, it was a relief to have Chandice go on about her own life; just from her brief interaction with my boys, I could imagine her daughter leaning into her classroom children with that same warm gleam. Getting to know Chandice a little bit was a welcomed distraction from the real reason she was here, although Lucas mostly pushed his food around his plate, would probably fill up on cheese sticks and Oreo cookies later after carefully checking the ingredients. Only Owen seemed to really love the meal, kicking his legs contentedly under the table. "Yummy stuffing." He would go on about that stuffing for a good year.

Chandice grinned at him. "You like?" She leaned into him as he happened to wind up sitting at her elbow. "Wait until you try my *pie*."

I expected Owen to look a little dubious. He didn't like pie. He would have preferred cake.

He grinned back.

Then my mother started to choke on her own stuffing, her eyes widening. Chandice in an instant was up and coming around the table to gently but purposely pound my mother's hunched back, and we were all reminded of the real reason this stranger was living in my mother's home. Only later, would I really think about that though, what it was like for this woman to move from one elderly person to the next, to follow through with one more awful slow demise. Before she brought back from the Bronx her own baking "tools", she improvised a birthday cake for me the following February, shaping flower petals with icing squeezed from a plastic sandwich bag, and edging the cake with the ridges of a paper towel. "She's very excited about it," my mother made a point of telling me. "You have to know how excited she is." In a rare moment, my mother could look past her resentment of this stranger, to her feelings—my mother did not want to see Chandice hurt. Maybe even she realized how all the baking might have literally been keeping Chandice herself from going crazy.

6

The problem with home-care agencies is that they set their own protocols. And the protocol of this agency was for their aides to be cycled out once a month to avoid caregiver burnout, so after only three weeks, the home-care agency called to say it was soon time for Chandice to take a break.

"Bullshit," Chandice said.

"But you *are* tired," I said.

She gave me one of her frowns. "What do you think would happen if another stranger now came in to take care of your mother? You think her mental state is bad *now*?"

I said nothing.

"Exactly."

Then she added, "I'm tired, yes. But I sleep around your mother's schedule," which I knew meant she often slept during the day so that she could be up with my mother nights.

We were talking in my mother's kitchen, where we seemed to have all our critical conversations. I already knew Chandice was irreplaceable. It was a knowing all intuitive; at this point in our trajectory, there was no turning back. And she knew as well as I did they were paying her a small fraction of what I was actually paying them—rather, what my mother was, as I was exercising my power of attorney over her accounts. Chandice and I agreed on a rate that satisfied us both, and I hoped would satisfy my mother, as much as I still kept an eagle eye on her bank accounts, wondering what would be left if my mother actually *did* live to be a hundred.

So Chandice and I hatched our plan: I would terminate my contract with the agency, claiming I had made other arrangements for my mother's care. Chandice would then terminate her own contract and return to the Bronx for the weekend; I would stay with my mother while my husband watched the boys. We were each circumventing a steep penalty for employing aides previously contracted with the agency. Desperate times call for desperate measures. My desperation would only intensify over those last months of my mother's life.

I looked forward to this time alone with my mother. I'd learned to turn off the baby monitor in her room so Chandice could not overhear our entire exchanges, but I still always felt as if we could not talk as freely as we always had.

As soon as Chandice left, the space of my mother's house seemed to open up around us. I imagined a soup lunch at her table in the sunroom, where we might see deer out her windows, and she'd complain again about how they "were just eating everything." That night, we'd sit by the fire in the living room, and I'd make her a light Scotch. Naively, I imagined we could fall back into how we'd always been together.

After driving Chandice up to the bus Saturday morning, I made my mother's breakfast and brought it into her room on a tray.

"Oh, you're such a good daughter!" she said, as I set the tray on her bed. "And such a relief to have that *person* gone.

I feel like I'm in my own home again!" she exclaimed, clapping her hands as she could when she was happy. She cracked her egg with her spoon and scooped out the white, leaving the yolk. "And so good to see you. Sit and tell me what's new."

My mother always had asked me that, what's new. Even though we talked regularly on the phone, when I visited, she could listen again to the same stories I'd already told her on the phone, about the boys playing "library," taking down all my books from the shelves. But I also could talk about myself—my frustration about being unable to write. And in this writing drought, she encouraged me in my other creative outlets, in my forays into drawing, collage and the fiber arts. "Sandy, you've always had so much talent," she'd tell me when I'd show her my latest work whatever that may be, as I had been showing her my drawings since I was a child. She would rave over my scribbles back then, tell me how I had an innate sense of design, knowing just how to balance lights against the darks. She would listen as I now listened to my own children, in that way she had of inhaling my whole presence. Early on, my mother saw in me what she saw in herself, and what I don't think her own mother could see in her daughter who gifted her "Night Garden."

It seemed so long ago since we'd been like this, when we had each other's full attention, as much as we seemed to be straining across a divide, me leaning out from the fragile rocking chair, her trying to pull herself up in bed so that she was sitting upright. I knew we would not have another time like this; it was my chance to talk to her about anything. Instead, I could only think to tell her about Owen's new parakeet, one he picked out himself, with unusual yellow markings. Owen for a long time had wanted a parakeet, and one day, truly on the spur of the moment, we stopped at Petco and bought one—the way you should never decide on pet ownership. We transported the little bird home in its lunchbox-like cardboard carrier, and I knew I'd consented to the parakeet for all the wrong reasons: to make things *better*. A desperation I saw for what it was, when we opened the cardboard box and the parakeet flapped its clipped wings in such panic, it flew off haphazardly, aimlessly, before we could get it into its cage.

I didn't tell her any of this. I only told her how Owen was trying to train the bird to sit on his finger.

"I do so miss seeing them," my mother said, and I promised to bring them to visit soon, though after Thanksgiving, I could not forget their look of horror when my mother began choking at the table.

Then my mother's eyes were drifting shut.

"Mom?"

Her head fell back awkwardly against her pillows. One hand twitched. She mumbled something, then awakened as if she could feel me watching her. Her eyes widened. She wiped her mouth on the sleeve of that pink sweater, and asked, "How do you like your new mattress?"

"My what?"

"In the tent. Your camping trip with Arthur."

Arthur. Her brother. Who died at seventeen. Some 80 odd years ago....

I knew she could awaken from dreams that could seem as real as reality. But this was the first time she was mixing up generations.

"I'm not camping," I said, irritably. But I was frightened. As I had been in the hospital after her concussion.

She laughed, embarrassed now. "Well, of course not." She looked down at her spoon, contemplating it, and it occurred to me that she was living her life in the third person. As if she was trying to tell herself a story. Trying to get to its end.

Then she asked, "Remind me where what's-her-name went again?"

I reminded her Chandice had gone home to the Bronx

for a couple of days.

"Well good. Because I just can't stand having someone around all the time!"

I didn't want to talk about Chandice. But I suddenly felt depleted, and didn't feel like talking about anything else either.

She reached for her coffee now. "So good to see you. So tell me."

"Tell you what?" A wave of exhaustion washed over me.

"Well, all what's going on. What's new."

Now she was awake and attentive, and it came over me suddenly—I wanted to cry. I wanted my *mom*. I wanted to tell her about how lost I'd become in my own space, in my own house, when the boys came home from school and I'd forget to empty their backpacks or sign permission slips for upcoming trips. When they would tell me about their day over snacks of Oreo cookies, and their voices travelled up to me as if from under water. I wanted to be able to tell her about what I knew she would understand, how my escaping out onto the porch was like her disappearing in a canoe across the lake. Unable myself to paddle off into a setting sun, I escaped to our front porch to drink wine capped off with the diazepam. And now I had started smoking again, hiding my butts in an old flowerpot. Even in winter, I'd sit out there wrapped in a blanket, listening to frozen trees creaking in the wind because for a few minutes I could afford to forget the things I would have to remember the next day: to check the balance in her checking account; order Chandice's food list from PeaPod; schedule physical therapist appointments; find an electrician for the broken kitchen light switch; call her doctor for a prescription renewal; schedule at-home bloodwork to monitor her Coumadin levels. Cloaked in a darkness alleviated only by the dull glow of the porch light, I could bask in my own utter despair and weep freely.

Blinking back tears, I stared into my coffee.

I was grateful when she pointed toward the window. "Oh, *look*, a deer!"

I turned to look. A large buck was eating the snowball bush, but for her it was as if she was seeing the rare one back in Vermont, caught again in our headlights. My vision blurred as I let the tears fall.

"Oh..." I managed, weakly, unable to muster any of her own exuberance. I wiped at eyes before turning back to her. I no longer could let her see me cry.

Alone with my mother for the first time since having a live-in aide, I found out exactly what nights were like for Chandice. What it was like listening to my mother all night long on the staticky baby monitor; far noisier than it ever was with my babies. The first part of the night she spent talking to the cats, asking them to please move over to the other side of the bed so that she could stretch out her legs. The rest of the night, I struggled with the volume, trying to tone down the static while still being able to hear if she tried to get out of bed.

At some point, I guess we both fell to sleep. But then I woke to her screaming "Sandy! *Saaaannnndy!*"

I sat bolt upright, my heart pounding.

I found her standing in the middle of her room, leaning on her walker.

"What? What is it?"

She turned to look at me. "What's the matter? What are you doing up?"

"Mom, you were screaming for me."

"I was?" She looked around as if she'd been dropped down into an alien space.

"Mom." *You don't remember calling out my name.*

"I don't know...It's so quiet. Why is it so quiet?"

I said because it was early on a Sunday morning. There was the first light, but the birds seemed not to have even awakened yet.

"Do me a favor, pull up my blinds?"

"Mom, it's not time to get up."

"Please, Sandy, just do as I ask." There was the same trembling terror in her voice as when she thought my father had been kidnapped.

I pulled up the blinds. Outside, the morning dew was a filmy light across her lawn.

She looked toward the windows, then said, "I know I'm in my house but I feel like I'm somewhere else."

The silence of the dawn pounded in my ears.

We both just stood there. Listening. To a silence that roared.

I suggested she get back into bed and try to sleep.

But she stayed rooted to the middle of her room. "I don't remember what I was doing..."

"Were you going to the bathroom?"

"Well, yes, I do need to go..."

She rolled her walker across the carpet. Smoothly, as Chandice taught me the trick of slicing open tennis balls to cup onto the wheels.

She went into the bathroom and shut the door, but without the lock, I was able to open the door a crack and watch her in the mirror, as she maneuvered the walker around the toilet. My concern was that she would have trouble getting herself up off the toilet, even with the commode. Which she did.

She sat back down heavily on the commode, head in her hands, talking to herself as she could. "Oh, what is wrong with me? And I'm so tired...tired, tired, *tired*!"

"Mom let me help you."

"Sandy?" she said, as if she'd already forgetting I was just outside the door. "Oh, Sandy...you don't need this."

We argued over the fact that I was her daughter, the reason I should be allowed to help her, and she argued the opposite, that she didn't want me to "see" her like this. She'd forgotten, of course, what I couldn't forget, how up close I'd already seen her.

"Oh, where is what's her name?" she asked irritably.

I reminded her, again, that Chandice had gone home to the Bronx.

"Well, when is she coming back?"

Talking to each other from opposite sides of a door, I realized neither of us felt safe any longer alone with each other. We both wanted Chandice to come back.

Sunday afternoon, I picked Chandice up from the bus, with that one large suitcase now full of bake pans, her own blender, and enormous vitamin bottles. She went into my mother's room as she had her first night, without taking off her coat. But this time when she took off her hat, my mother said, "Your hair!"

Chandice threw back her head and laughed. "Yes! I got it cut!"

Relieved, I laughed too; my mother actually remembered what Chandice looked like from before she left.

7

Chandice rarely took days off after that. If she did, she entrusted one of her colleagues from the Bronx to come down and care for my mother, even though she would chastise them when she returned to find my mother's bedsores aggravated, and for the mess they might leave in the kitchen.

When I told her about how my mother had been up in the middle of the night, Chandice was unfazed. "Well, yes. And she also sometimes barks in her sleep too."

My mother barks?

"If not calling for her mother."

I don't know what surprised me more, the barking or my mother calling out for her own mother—once I had asked if she was close to her mother, and she'd answered with a definite "No." She then followed up with what she'd always believed, that my grandmother had never gotten over the death of her first-born son. But even before Arthur died, before my grandmother evidently retreated into her chamber of grief, my mother remembered being left in the care of a nurse. How she was "left to cry and cry." After my mother died, I would come across a crumbling album in the deep recesses of the attic, with the first candid shots I'd ever seen of her—only one is of her with my grandmother, in a hammock up at Lake Sunapee; my grandmother is holding my mother on her lap, but staring stoically into the distance; her thoughts seemingly elsewhere. In the other photos it is a nurse who holds my mother, and often my mother is reaching her hands out as if she wants to get down. The expression on the nurse's face, a detachment similar to my grandmother's.

One candid is of my mother alone, outside of anyone's grasp. She is about four and standing on a beach. She is reaching her small hands up into the wind, as if trying to catch it. Outside of my wailing on the day she died, finding this photograph is one of the few other times I was reduced to real, relentless weeping.

Finding those photos was when I began to consider my mother as whole being, in the absence of her aura, of the way she had always surrounded me. Even though I grew up with things from her childhood—a pair of china terriers, one with a broken tail that wound up in own china animal collection, and her baby doll with the china head propped up on a shelf—I'd never really thought about my mother as a child, and even less so, as a daughter.

Outside of the photos, and the few stories she'd told me again and again, I knew little of her true relationship with her own mother beyond what I remember about our visits every Sunday after Church. We also regularly visited my mother's godmother, and I remember those visits in stark contrast. Unlike my grandmother, Aunt Didi would talk and laugh and had a Siamese cat. Before the cat, she'd been devoted to a pet boa constrictor; my mother told me how she'd gotten the snake because she could not bear to have another dog after her beloved German Shepherd, Ricky, died. When the snake died, she could not bear another snake, and so she got a cat instead, who rarely came out for strangers—I would spend long moments peering at Simi's dark stern face where he crouched under Aunt Didi's bed. When I wasn't watching the cat watch me, I sought out the little treasures in a bottom desk drawer, where Aunt Didi kept an odd messy assortment of half-burned candles, an old watch, decks of cards, and my favorite, a box with a magnetic mouse. I remember the sound of Aunt Didi's voice, how she could talk rapidly and animatedly, as I sat on the worn oriental rug, moving the magnet under the box so that the mouse would chase a wedge of cheese.

These visits were filled with light and pattern, unlike my grandmother's: everything as green as moss, the living room cast in a stagnant watery light. She no longer lived in the house where my mother grew up on Staten Island, on Prospect Avenue, but in an apartment in a three-story house—I remember the layout well. The long hallway, with the kitchen off to the right. Then the aide's room at one end of the hall, and my grandmother's at the other, the only room with real sun coming in, shimmering across her pink satin quilt.

When we arrived, my grandmother was always seated at the far end of a living room couch, in reach of her water glass on the side table. She had a linen handkerchief crumpled in one hand or tucked up a sleeve. It's her legs I remember best; they were like two tree trunks rooted in thick tan-colored orthopedic shoes. My grandmother's face seemed to sag with the weight of her own jowls. But what was a never-ending fascination for me was her hair— wound up, always, into a complicated bun with countless hair pins. Her hair never went gray, and I always yearned to see it unfurl down her back.

There was little in the way of real conversation, and I often drifted into the small side room, with the collection of china blue jays lining her desk, and the china cabinet with the yellow-and-black tea set that eventually would make its way into my mother's kitchen hutch. To play with, there was that fold-up paper dollhouse, and oddly, a box of tiny naked plastic babies. I'd fan open the dollhouse to make the babies sit on the pop-up toilet or cook at the stove. When I was especially bored, I'd repeatedly open and close the dollhouse, just to watch all the furniture pop up. There was no door to this room, so I could easily hear my mother repeatedly asking if she could get my grandmother anything, a glass of water or tea? Any real conversation seemed saved for the live-in aide, when my mother would go into the kitchen to discuss, I assume, my grandmother, in hushed tones, leaving my father to talk to my grandmother about the beautiful weather we've been having, or how much we needed this rain. I'd gather up the tiny plastic babies, cup them in my hands and shake them so that their hard little bodies clattered.

When once I played Parcheesi with my grandmother was the only time I ever visited her alone, and I can still wonder at my mother's intent—maybe it was to forge a relationship between grandmother and grandchild that otherwise I only can recall from photographs. Although in all the photos of us, my grandmother seems staged, settled into a fold-up chair out on our front stoop while I'm playing in the grass, the sun glistening off her pale nylon stockings, off those tree-trunk legs; on our living-room couch watching me open her birthday present. My grandmother is staring vacantly, as if wondering what she'd given me. No doubt my mother had bought and wrapped the present for her, just as I would wind up doing with the boys' presents from Gramma.

For this odd visit alone with my grandmother, I don't know where my mother went while I was there. She couldn't have gone far; I was only eight or nine. We did not live close by, so perhaps she was sitting out in the car. Or maybe she was actually there, in the kitchen again, talking with the aide. Whatever the case, my impression was indeed of being *left* there, to sit opposite my grandmother across a fold-up TV tray. I don't remember us talking. Only the click of her nails on the Parcheesi board, and my feeling somehow that I was there to entertain her—most certainly, I was not there of my own volition. I was there as an act of duty, though I remember being pleasantly surprised by the swift way my grandmother could roll the dice so that they spun across the board.

I did not go there alone again, and I can wonder now whether my spending a long drawn out afternoon with my grandmother wasn't so much about me as it was about my mother trying to please her mother. As she seemed to have been trying to please her with the gift of the "Night Garden," though I don't remember it ever hanging in my grandmother's apartment, nor how my mother came into possession of it again, most likely after my grandmother died. And there was nothing celebratory or significant about, years later, her gifting the painting to me, after happening on it while cleaning out the storeroom in the attic, pulling things out only to put them all back as periodically she would do. Besides those daguerreotypes and old lace we'd found when she originally inherited the house, there were my father's boxes of manuscripts and commencement cap and gown; the antique dish rack that hung in the hall of the Staten Island house; her old fondue dish from the faculty parties she threw for my father; and stacked against one wall, her oldest paintings, where she didn't care whether they warped from the intense heat under the eaves. Ones she thought were "no good," and whose canvases she'd always planned to tear off so she could reuse the stretchers.

She found "Night Garden" hidden behind the stack of large old paintings, a small painting in a thick wooden frame. She seemed surprised by it, having forgotten it was buried behind all those other old paintings, all these years. "Goodness..." she said, holding it out in front of her, looking at it quizzically.

She laughed. "Poor Mother. She couldn't make anything

of it."

How exactly did my grandmother respond to such a dark painting, its flowers so obscured? She might have laughed a little, a warbling laugh, a mix of confusion and even embarrassment at not being able to understand: goodness, why so dark, and what is that odd shape going up the corner? That surprise of stark white that looks almost like a mistake? Or was it a conscious surrendering of the control my mother was trying to maintain in the painting? An abstracted area where my mother seemed unable to resist breaking out and away from that, from trying to paint flowers that would please her mother?

My mother offered the painting to me as casually as she did other things we pulled out, the old lamp I remembered from my grandmother's hall table, and a punch bowl, as if I would ever serve punch. "But don't take it if you don't like it."

I wasn't sure whether I was supposed to like the painting or not; she clearly was not particularly fond of it herself. But it was also clear to me that she bore the hurt of her mother's dislike of it. To this day, I don't know how to feel about "Night Garden" as a painting– if it were a short story, I'd critique the point of view as inconsistent: on the one hand it was "written" in the distant first person, with the perfectly shaped pink flower. On the other hand, it was an up-close colloquial first person, especially with the stark splash of white up one corner. Either way, I took the painting; it hung in my bedroom in Brooklyn, then when I married, migrated to our house on Long Island.

I would not think to take down "Night Garden" from where it hangs on our bedroom wall until I was writing this chapter and I would find its title scrawled on the back. To examine the painting more closely, I brought it over to the window—in the dark of the garden, what I'd always assumed was a pitch black, there is the glint of blue. Those black areas are actually varying hues of blue. I now can imagine she'd been trying for how flora might look in moonlight, but so belabored the blue, its original brilliance became muddied. The layers are so thick, they have cracked in places. And I'd always assumed it was unsigned. Now I saw the faint shadow of a signature and date, 1960 in the lower right corner; I'd assumed she'd painted it when she was much younger, still struggling to find her statement as an artist—she was already in her forties and married. Still, she'd signed it simply "Betty Sloan" rather than Elizabeth Sloan Tyler. She signed it as her mother's daughter rather than as the artist she was.

What I thought was one of her bright "notes" she liked to add to her paintings, I saw now was where the paint had chipped—the bright note was actually another layer showing through. Either she'd painted over some old painting she didn't like, or her first attempt had not been a night garden but one in full sunlight. One with the vibrant colors of her cubist phase, her Verrazano paintings of green and orange, but with her mother, she had felt she needed to suppress.

The idea of chipping away at the whole painting was hard to resist. Because I wanted to get at the *truth* of the painting—the inner workings of my mother. And not *as* my mother. Not even as her mother's daughter. But as the complex woman who by the time she painted "Night Garden," was newly married, not yet pregnant, and wrestling with that inner obsession of artists: to be understood. To be *known*. As maybe in those last years of her life I was getting to know her in just that, in her diminished capacity to be there in the only way I'd ever known her, as my mother.

Still, if not able to understand "Night Garden," my grandmother seemed to have been able to at least honor this expressive force in my mother, one not to be tamed, when she gave in to my mother's pleading to go away to boarding school at Northfield Mount Hermon. My mother always credited my grandmother for having the prescience to know she would flourish there in a way she couldn't at the small stifling private school on Staten Island—as I credited my mother for taking me out of that same small stifling school to move me into the large public school where I first flourished as a writer. And therein lay perhaps my real connection to my mother: her understanding of me in a way she had mostly gone misunderstood.

8

I hated to admit that this stranger in my mother's house was no longer that, a stranger. But I began to practice what Chandice preached: to not reason with my mother. When she called because she'd been arrested—"just because I was feeding the hungry!"—I assured her that Chandice would be coming shortly to take her home (wheeling her out of "jail" into the living room). When she called to tell me she was locked in a church, I told her I'd send one of the parishioners to pick her up. When she told me she was "waiting and waiting" in the dental chair, I told her that I believed her when she insisted I did not. It became second nature for me to lie about the truth of things, as there no longer was a familiar context of us as the mother and daughter who used to talk on the phone over lunch. Over bowls of soup, from our two points on the map.

Seeing my mother now became less about us, than my glimpsing what it really was like between her and Chandice, how well-practiced she was in her profession. She may have had a whole other life—which she did—outside the walls of my mother's house, with a daughter in Jamaica. She may have had aspirations to one day open her own bakery, a life of her own beyond leading the fragile volatile elderly through their last demise, this final slow disaster. But within these walls of my mother's house, she was entirely in her element. I would come to trust Chandice's advice implicitly, because this strong, ultimately compassionate, woman had earned the right to pride herself on how she was able to rehydrate wrinkled dry skin with daily baby oil rubs; pamper aching arthritic feet with Epson salt soaks; ease bedsores with her most trusted barrier cream Calmoseptine, the one she swore by with all of her demented incontinent patients; on styling my mother's gray-gone-white hair so she might feel beautiful. And I would do as I was told, hide my mother's pill bottles behind her empty red kitchen tins, as she no longer could keep track of her own dosages. I'd take away her checkbooks where she kept them in her top bureau drawer, after Chandice caught her writing out a check to Save the Children dated 1939 and for $50,000 rather than $50. I removed the stash of cash she kept in the coffee can in her closet, after she was swindled of $600 from a chimney company. I would do all these things as surreptitiously as I'd removed the lock from her bedroom door.

I remember for one visit in particular, Chandice asked me to pick up Epson salts and Baking Soda. My mother's toenails were so tough and hard, she wanted to soften them in foot bath before attempting to cut them.

"Her feet will be smooth as a baby's bottom," she said, opening the bag of salts. She was wearing a sweater I recognized as my mother's, a yellow knit she used to wear when we went out to dinner, dressing it up with a neck scarf or one of her pendants. My mother now mostly wore that pink Sherpa sweater I'd given her for her birthday, its Sherpa long since matted, and she could obsess about getting rid of her clothes: "I'm going to be gone soon anyway, someone might as well enjoy them." So on good days, when she was on good terms with Chandice, she evidently allowed her to pick what she liked from her closet —the very person she once did not want touching her clothes.

Chandice filled a large steel mixing bowl with water to soak my mother's feet, one she found as easily as if this were her own kitchen. Like the blender, I'd forgotten my mother even owned the bowl. She poured the salts into the bowl, adding several tablespoons of baking soda. She could have been mixing a batter for another cake. Such moments, when I was standing in what should have been my mother's kitchen, I was able to feel that, my mother's angst about things out of their rightful place, her pots stacked haphazardly beneath the butcher's block table; her fruit bowl moved from the table to the top of the microwave to store potatoes, her decorative ceramic teapot actually being used to brew tea. In those moments, I *was* taking my mother's side, moments when I was bereft and lost amongst things so familiar, they only had ever been overlooked.

At the same time, I was deeply grateful to Chandice; ever since her hip replacement, my mother had complained about being unable to bend down to cut her toenails, and I'd been tormented by the fact that I should be cutting them for her. But I had trouble just looking at my mother's toenails—ragged as the weathered mineral rocks my boys would find every summer in the New Hampshire Polar Bear caves, though not nearly as . . . magnificent.

Chandice settled my mother out in the sunroom, in her favorite Ikea chair. She had styled her hair; Chandice had taken to not only washing and curling her hair, but cutting it as well.

"Isn't she beautiful?" Chandice asked, the first time I remember her cutting my mother's hair after she finally had those stitches removed.

I had just arrived, and stood in the bedroom doorway, entranced by this scene: my mother sitting on the edge of her bed, surrounded by her white hair fallen in half-moons.

Chandice held up a hand mirror for her. I expected my mother to become enraged; she rarely came home from the hair salon satisfied—either her hair was cut too short so she "looked like a man," or uneven as if they'd taken a "hacksaw" to it. If Chandice were a real hair dresser, my mother would have switched to another; her hair was teased out in a way she despised, so that her head looked like newly spun cotton candy.

What I had expected was wrath. Instead, my mother looked blankly at herself. She could have been staring out a window. "Oh, I'm just *gorgeous*."

As Chandice carried the steel bowl out to where my mother sat, I longed now as I had then, to press down my mother's hair so that she didn't look quite so coiffed, so ridiculous. Of course, I didn't, afraid of rattling this precarious calm. I knew how the temperature between them could shift from moment to moment, as when my mother found Chandice mixing batter in her large red Kitchen Aide bowl. "This is *my* kitchen!" my mother had screeched, stamping her walker on the old linoleum floor. Chandice had only smiled, holding out the wooden spoon for my mother to taste the batter. "But I'm making your favorite, Mrs. Tyler. Chocolate layered cake." My mother had licked her lips. She'd stuck her finger into the bowl to swoop out a large dollop. "As long as you clean up this mess."

Chandice tucked my mother's ugly feet into the mixing bowl. I glimpsed a big mineral rock-like toe, nauseated.

My mother started to protest, taking out her feet, her toes dripping.

"But what did I say...this will make your feet smooth as..." Chandice waited, her arms in the air like a school teacher's.

My mother looked up at her, a confused child being asked what did one plus one equal.

"A baaaaby's booooootom!" Chandice sang.

My mother obediently dropped her feet back into the

water. She gazed down at her feet, wiggling her toes. I had never known her to go for even a single pedicure.

My mother then looked at Chandice as appraisingly as she only ever had looked at me: "That sweater. It's becoming on you."

Becoming.

I stood there, as the earth seemed to shift again. As if I could actually feel the tectonic shift of the earth's plates, at once subtle but pronounced. I must have made some kind of noise, a gasp or a hiccup, because Chandice looked up from my mother's feet. At me.

I had to look away. From them both. From my mother with her ridiculous hair and Chandice crouched over my mother's mixing bowl of Epson salts, her large hands massaging my mother's ugly arthritic feet.

I left the room.

I found myself wandering into my mother's bedroom, where I stood in the middle of it; everything was neatly folded and put away. In a way my mother didn't seem to object to anymore.

I needed to move. Over to the open window to shut it.

"Please don't."

Chandice was standing in the doorway. She came over and stood with me by the window.

"Don't shut the window."

She told me how my mother complained that she was imprisoned without it open.

My first instinct: to reason. "It's below freezing out. It's sending the thermostat up."

She put her hands together in a steeple. *"Please."*

And then I saw it: my mother wanted windows open Chandice dared not close. Just as she might very well later accuse Chandice of "stealing" that very same sweater.

Chandice took ahold of that sweater now, as it hung open on her, too small to button closed. "Does this bother you?"

"No...." I said, knowing how much it did.

"You know, your mother called me nigger."

Nigger? I went white with horror and embarrassment.

Chandice evidently had refused to leave my mother's room, when again my mother was demanding her "privacy."

But no. I'd never known my mother to use that word. My mother was not a racist. "That's not my mother."

"I know it's not—that's my point. The only reason I'm even telling you. What I've been saying all along."

In my head I was asking how could my mother be reduced to that? Where did that word come from, one that I knew she would not want in her vocabulary? But then I envisioned my mother sitting out there in her Ikea chair, with her feet in the tepid water. The way she could stare blankly, flip through the same catalogue over and over, not remembering the previous page.

"It's the disease," I said.

Chandice nodded in her knowing way.

And Chandice did know, had already found out—what my mother was *really* like. Not in the way I had always known my mother. When she'd take me in to her studio to ask my opinion of her latest paintings, when she'd marvel at me in dressing room mirrors; not the mother who at times knew me better than I knew myself, when she realized I was actually "afraid of life." Not in the way I would come to know my mother after she was gone, when I would discover that small tin of oil paints, and imagine her adrift in that rowboat. When I would discover those snippets of brilliant blond hair from when she was a little girl and wore her hair pulled back in a large awkward bow, in a portrait of her with my grandmother. When I would start to think about my mother not just as a mother, but as a daughter herself.

Chandice was coming to know my mother as she was in the now, in this new, baffling present, at once more like herself and entirely not herself at all. The one who needed her window open in 20-degree weather; ate Cajun shrimp; watched Jeopardy when she'd only ever watched Channel 13, and would call to tell me to turn on a special about the Picasso sculpture exhibit; who one day could complain to "them" that she would start to "cackle like a chicken" if she was fed any more chicken, only to turn around the next day, when Chandice grilled her a steak instead, to snap, "I only want to eat chicken. Nothing but chicken!"

My mother would only become more tenacious in her tastes and distastes and could drive both me and Chandice to distraction. But as the months wore on, Chandice could also say to me, "You know I really *admire* your mother." And in that remark, I deeply appreciated Chandice's real wisdom, even if it may have been a practiced one, in how she was able to look past—or *through*—the clouded, confused, surface of my mother, to her true veneer. Especially in my mother's last weeks when, however weakened, her battle for control over *her* life, reined. When she'd lift a weak shaky hand to point at her glass on the bedside table. "*Please.* Use a *coaster.*"

And so, the very thing that could drive us both to distraction, Chandice admired: my mother's emboldened spirit, the one that all her life propelled her back time and again to the canvas. The same one that sent her riding down a mountain in a lightning storm, or to stand out at the edge of the ocean and exude, "Look at that *sky*!" My mother right up to her dying day, plunged fearlessly forward into life, in the way she'd plunge into the lake, into the cold October waters at the bay. It was this spirit that enabled her to live independently for so long, what would become, quite literally, the one thing still keeping her alive. Even in all her late-stage confusion, she could say what she had been saying all along: "I *love* this earth. I do not want to leave it!"

9

Except for Christmas, I don't think I returned with the boys until their spring break. When we arrived, my mother was still in bed. Chandice disappeared into my mother's bedroom to help her get dressed, and I ushered the boys out to the sunroom so they wouldn't have to hear my mother chastising Chandice for not getting her up earlier.

The boys sat side by side on the couch, each with their new little hand-held game consoles, the Nintendo DS that they got for Christmas. That was the last time they'd seen their grandmother, when they'd opened presents she'd picked out from her catalogues, ones she had no memory of ordering for them in the first place. A large globe puzzle toy she'd helped Owen dismantle wound up in a jumbled heap in her lap, with her complaining how could anyone manufacture such a "frustrating" toy. For Lucas, she'd ordered a chemistry set that held his attention long enough for him to set up the little glass tubes on the coffee table, before he returned to whatever game he was playing on his new DS.

Lucas hid behind it then as he did now, poking at the screen with the little stylus, as Chandice helped my mother to manipulate her walker down the single step into the sunroom. Owen watched Grandma as unabashed as he had from behind his rock at the lake when she'd been scooting along the dock on her bottom.

My mother now only made the trek to the sunroom when the boys visited, even though she was faithfully still working with a home physical therapist to strengthen her weakening legs. She'd put on makeup, however caked and uneven her foundation appeared. Chandice had even styled her hair. My mother still could make a real effort for her grandsons, although by the time she arrived in the sunroom—and it could feel like that, an arrival—her shirt was riding up her back and pants askew as if she had arrived after some long commute.

Lucas looked up from his screen long enough to gape at his grandmother's cotton-candy hair.

Then there was her trek across the sunroom, to the enormous recliner that now replaced her beloved Ikea chair. "It's time," Chandice had said, when my mother no longer could sit comfortably in any of her house chairs, and she insisted I buy the monstrous faux leather thing. As she would insist a few months later, about the hospital bed that would replace her four poster one.

"Gramma, your chair is ginormous," Owen said. He had climbed into it and was playing with the lever.

"Is that *my* chair?" My mother said. "Well, if it is, it's awfully ugly."

"You could *live* in this chair," Owen said. "You could like set up a table and eat in it."

"Well, I wouldn't like to live in a chair. But I'm ready to sit in it," she said, gesturing for Owen to move. "Because I'm very, very *old!*" Then she laughed. "Don't *ever* grow old!"

Chandice and I stabilized my mother as we lowered her into the ginormous ugly chair. I couldn't help marveling at this new addition—how out of place aesthetically it was in my mother's home. Never in her right mind, would she have bought such an "ugly" chair for herself.

Once settled, she looked even smaller than Owen had in the chair, especially with the throw Chandice draped over her legs so only her yellow socks showed, bobbing there like buoys, a pair of nonskid hospital ones she'd collected over the years and Chandice insisted she wear.

She looked over at her grandsons sitting on the couch. "It's so good to *seeeee* you! Tell me what's *new*!"

There was a time when the boys would have been clambering into her lap to tell her about all that was "new." About the frog Lucas won at school, the fort Owen was building in our backyard.

Lucas didn't answer. He hunched down farther behind his DS.

Owen though, got up to pick up the cat's toy from the floor.

"Does Sammy still play with this?" he asked, swinging the wire with a little stuffed mouse at the end of it.

Sammy was the male cat (whom later, when I had to take him to the vet, I would find out was really a girl).

"Sammy?" My mother ran her finger under her chin. "Oh, well..." as if forgetting she had cats at all.

"Guess what," Chandice announced. "I made strawberry shortcake."

"Cake!" Owen exclaimed, clapping. "Is it someone's birthday?" Owen asked. "My birthday is in two weeks!" he said, holding up two fingers.

Chandice made so many cakes, it seemed always someone's birthday even when it wasn't, and I was not entirely surprised Chandice had offered to bake Owen's cake. Actually, it was less an offer than another announcement. Earlier that week when I'd come out alone, we were in my mother's kitchen. "I will make Owen's cake."

I was unpacking a bag from CVS, and Chandice was lining up the items on the counter, mentally checking whether I'd remembered everything: the Depends, Ocuvite,

Epson salts, Calcium, skin lotion, baby shampoo.

I should have been grateful, I suppose, not to have to bake a cake myself, especially as baking was far from my forte. I wasn't feeling grateful. Because *I did not want her baking my son's cake.*

"That would be great," I said, wondering why I could never say no to Chandice, even as she'd insist I spend $30 a week on frozen shrimp, what my mother would have deemed "outrageous." *What would she think of the way I was spending her money?*

"I'll make it in the shape of a football. He plays football, doesn't he?"

I hated that my boys played football. It was a ridiculous spectacle, these mere children out on the field in their heavy gear, a bunch of stupefied beetles bumping into each other.

"You just have to find me a cake mold in a football shape."

"It's almost Owen's birthday?" My mother now asked in utter surprise. "Sandy, why didn't you remind me?"

I clenched my teeth and hoped they wouldn't crack. Just last week I'd helped her to wrap the nerf gun I'd already bought as her present. "Why do you want to buy him guns?" she'd asked. She'd wanted to buy him some other educational toy from one of her museum catalogues. I'd finally talked her into what he really wanted, the latest and greatest, The Nerf E-Strike Disruptor Something or Other.

Chandice began cutting the cake with a tarnished old cake knife, a piece of silver I must have forgotten to hide. Owen rattled on about the party "Mommy" was planning, this year, a treasure hunt with a Spider-Man theme.

My mother asked him who was Spider-Man, and Owen rambled on as he was known to do. I welcomed his white noise as I tried to filter my thoughts: where am I going to find a cake pan in the shape of a football? Did they even sell them on Amazon, or was I going to have to trek all over Long Island, to Michaels, and Target, and Walmart? If I was smart, as my husband suggested, I would have booked a room at Chucky Cheese for a couple of hundred bucks and been done with it. But our boys always had big plans for their birthdays, and this year, Owen wanted to have an elaborate Spide-Man treasure hunt. I would be up late the next few nights, researching not just football molds, but Spider-Man trinkets, yoyos, stickers.

And now my mother: Oh, how she couldn't wait for his party! It sounded like "such fun!" And what would he like for his birthday? She asked Chandice to go get her basket of catalogues, and together she and Owen went through the toy ones until he picked out exactly what we'd already ordered for him. "Why would you ever want and go and shoot anyone?"

"It's a *toy*, Gramma," Owen said.

"Well, if it's what you really want, you should have it," she said, touching his cheek. "But we need to order it today so it comes in time for your birthday."

I took the catalogue, promised her I would order it, to avoid us buying duplicate guns.

What I began to realize on this trajectory, with all its sharp curves, was that there were many firsts. That summer would be the first when she was unable withstand the trip up to New Hampshire; I remember standing out on the dock at dusk our first night, staring down into my own shadow. The following Christmas was the first my mother was unable to wake up with us to watch the boys open their stocking presents. And now another first, missing her grandson's birthday.

My mother had driven up every year for their parties, and when I started worrying about her driving, I would pick her up. I can't say she was ever really able to help me with these parties, beyond filling the goody bags with party favors. But I could not imagine these parties without her; she was as integral as my elaborate decorations, and she might go around the table to fuss with the napkins or cups, to upright a fallen accordion paper centerpiece. One year, I had the idea for them to play Spiderweb, my favorite game from my own birthday parties; every year, my mother wound ball after ball of string in and around all the furniture up in our guest room. At the end of each string she'd wrapped a small present so that every child went home with their own little gift—my favorite, one year, kiddy dolls that popped out of plastic tulips. But just as you can't finally recreate the past, neither can you duplicate the experience of a favorite game—Spiderweb that year was a bust, and my mother and I would wonder where we had gone wrong. "We probably shouldn't have done it in the living room," she said, where there were too many obstacles. Whatever the reason, we hadn't anticipated some kids would break down crying because they got tangled up in their strings. Needless to say, we never tried the Spiderweb game again, though as time passed my mother and I could laugh about what a flub it was.

The cake wasn't in the shape of a football after all, as I never could find the football mold, but Chandice decorated the cake with an admirable rendition of one.

When it came time to cut the cake, Owen told everyone about how Chandice had made it, the "lady" who was taking care of his Gramma.

"What's wrong with your Grandma?" one of his friends asked.

The noise around the table ceased just like that. The boys stopped spinning their Spider-Man key chains, stopped punching the balloons dangling from the chandelier. They grew as still as they had when they'd discover a dead sparrow during their treasure hunt out in the yard. They had crouched in a circle around it, in a quiet not exactly reverent, but as solemnly curious as their silence now. There was only the slight rustling of restless knees against the paper cloth.

I was replenishing juice in their Spider-Man cups. I still had not talked to Lucas or Owen about what was "wrong" with their Gramma, why she needed taking care of in the first place. I never finally would. Just as I hoped they'd never find out about the flowerpot of cigarette butts accumulating on the porch that I'd tucked under the chair.

It was only Lucas who ever asked if Gramma was going to die. But that was long before she'd become this disabled, when he'd first asked about the tombstones. Before my mother began to recede. Before it was no longer a question in need of asking.

I waited for Owen's answer.

He grew thoughtful. Then he frowned at his friends, at their foolish question. "Well...she's just very, very, *old*," he said. "Don't *ever* grow old!"

10

My mother would die exactly one week following Owen's next birthday. She would be bedridden, her heart most likely already beginning to fail, and Chandice would not be doing any more baking. I would book Owen's party at a local paintball outdoor arena, where he would have a Carvel cake inside a bunker in a muddy field. Inside that tin shed, the noise of ten boys around a fold-up table would literally ring hollow. It can seem remarkable, my not having the prescience to realize my mother was already actively dying. But in that final year, I moved through my days as if through a mirage. Through the murky layers of reflections and shadows of staring down into the lake, when as a child I'd stand at the end of the dock, trying to make out the tangible, the schools of minnows in that watery undulating world.

There are those moments, however, that do now rise to the surface: my mother's fixation her last summer, on the flower box I'd set up on the porch railing where she could see it from her bedroom window. Every single time I talked to her on the phone, she'd remind me "what joy" it brought her. She'd remark on the brilliant pink of the Picasso geraniums, how "gorgeous" they were, set against the violet purple of the bluebells, and she could have been remarking on the sky at dusk, the way those colors could wind up in another painting.

Another moment: we were waiting to see her orthopedist, and I remember her pointing a crooked arthritic finger at a neon blue-and-yellow fish circling a large tank in the middle of the waiting room. "Oh, look at *that* one!"

I had wheeled her around so that she could face the voluminous salt-water tank, the centerpiece of the waiting room. Every fish that swam into her view was as remarkable as if swimming into her line of vision for the first time. "Oh look at that one, with the pink fins!" she'd explain, as the pink-finned fish circled the tank for maybe the millionth time since we'd signed in for our appointment.

She had fallen and broken her wrist, in a rare moment when Chandice cracked. "That's dangerous," Chandice had warned her when my mother, without her walker, was taking her pants off in her walk-in closet. "I'm not an invalid!" my mother had screeched, pulverizing Chandice long enough for her to turn away—and for my mother to fall.

Waiting in the waiting room with the big tank, my mother could not remember falling, and would ask over and over why she was wearing this unwieldy splint contraption. But she would then forget, as she would marvel at the same fish, and I would revel in her marveling, as I had with my father watching the ducks—with my kids, when we'd take them to the aquarium. "Look at that one," I'd exclaimed, as the blue-and-yellow striped fellow swam back into view. As if for the first time.

"Do you still find moments when you two can enjoy each other as you used to?" my therapist once asked. Well, perhaps the answer was no. At least not in the way we used to, though in a new way. In the redundancy of these momentary joys, those memory lapses that rendered everything new, when I could find some relief from my exhaustion in my mother's fresh delight.

My mother's stroke would only exacerbate my mother's mental deficits. One evidently mild, that supposedly left only a slight deficit in her left eye, but I soon realized may have altered her memory forever. One whose detriment made itself known on the drive home from the hospital, when she kept asking if we couldn't stop for the night at a hotel—she no longer recognized a single landmark. Not the church where I was married, not the pond where she would seek out the mated pair of swans, not the sight of her own home as we pulled into her gravel driveway.

I don't think I fully registered the severity of this memory impairment until I was visiting soon after she was discharged, and she remarked, "Well, this is such a lovely place."

I'd lit a fire in her living room. She sat in front of it, in her wheelchair. And then she said, "It's a shame we can't stay longer" what she often said when we'd be vacationing in New England, at some bed-and-breakfast, a country inn, at a lake cottage when we went with the children.

I made myself laugh. "Well, you can stay as long as you like. It's your home."

She looked over at me and laughed too. "Well, of course it's *not*..."

I felt suddenly light-headed. My palms began to sweat. I forgot to breathe. "This is your happy house."

She continued to laugh. In that silent way that she now could weep. "My what house?" Then she was peering across the room at the hutch, at her collection of hand-painted dishes. "Well, aren't those pretty."

Pretty.

I reminded her of the stories she had told me, of watching her Aunt Bell Bell as a child paint those daffodils and roses with tiny brushes, how even then, she couldn't have imagined painting anything so delicate.

She ran a finger under her chin in that way she could. "Oh?"

"Mom, you really don't recognize these dishes?"

She laughed again. *"No, I don't recognize those dishes..."* she said, mimicking me.

I wheeled her into the kitchen.

"Well, yes, it's all very lovely..."

"This is your *kitchen*."

She gave me an amused look as if this had become a game, and then said, "Well, if you say so. You always did have the last word..."

"This isn't my opinion. It's a fact."

Chandice I knew, could hear us from her room where she would retreat now, to give us time together. But I didn't care if she did hear me talking like this. *Reasoning* with my mother....

I wheeled her out to her studio. I parked her in the doorway. I went and stood in the middle of the vast space, turned on the floodlights so they spotlit her canvases. "Who painted these?"

She laughed and laughed, that silence welling up so that her chest shook. "Well, I don't know, Dear, but they're not half bad...."

"*Mom.*"

Doubt flickered across her face. She rubbed her finger under her chin. "Well...I should be going. I left the windows open...." She let her hand drop heavily into her lap. "But I'm just exhausted..."

Chandice was there. She materialized as she could. "You can lay down before you go."

"Just for a few minutes. It's going to rain, and it will ruin the sills..."

"Sandy will shut them for you." She glanced at me. There was that familiar frown, though now one tinged with a sadness. And compassion. For me.

From that point on, my mother never felt at home. Because she no longer was sure of where she was at any given moment, she was often restive. Lying in her own bedroom, she was only "napping" before her "long drive," worrying again that she'd left all her windows open "back home." And she could vent about that, how tired she was of all the travelling, of having to stay in so many different, foreign places. However "lovely" they might be, increasingly she only wanted to go home. "I just want to go *home*!"

Worse than the restive was her paranoia and hallucinations, now intensified; I talked her down off cliffs; out of true panic and fear, when she was lost in a city with no money, no place to live, no food; shady men walked back and forth through her bedroom. Then there was the night she screamed to me on the phone that she was being tortured with the andirons up her rectum—screamed in pain for me to "make them stop! Make them stop!"

Soon after the stroke, she was back in the hospital with aspiration pneumonia, and from then on, Chandice would have to thicken all liquids to the consistency of pureed soup. At the time though, there was little talk of her actually being able to survive the pneumonia, when her blood pressure plummeted to 58/40, her pulse 30—occasionally flatlining—and I was told she had anywhere from a few hours to 48 to live. When there had been only two options: the invasive, a line into her neck, or the less invasive, powerful IV antibiotics. Neither which her doctor expected to work.

Still, as her daughter, and healthcare proxy agent, I was faced with real decisions. I opted for the IV antibiotics, to assure myself that I was not deciding my mother's fate.

They agreed to the antibiotic route, I knew, only to compassionately appease a grown daughter suddenly reduced to a blubbering child, in the middle of the emergency room. So they admitted my mother into a private hospital room at the very end of the hall, what I referred to as the "death" room. There was a comfortable rocking chair, and an expansive tray of coffee and snacks the staff rolls in for "families" keeping deathwatch.

I *was* her family.

And I was not hungry.

I was only interested at being at my mother's bedside. I pulled up the rocking chair so I could lean over her bedrail. She slept as deeply as if she'd fallen into a cavernous crater, breathing harrowing breaths. I felt I should be memorizing her, the sharp distinctive slope of her nose, the birthmark on her forehead, a pale paper moon against an early morning sky.

For several hours I sat alone, rocking. Watching. Listening. The coffee carafes went untouched.

Occasionally a nurse popped in, but no doctors until several hours later; the same doctor who in emergency had told me point blank that the antibiotics would not work.

He checked her blood pressure.

It was back up. 110.

He looked at me as if to say, "Wow."

And I said, "You didn't expect this."

He shook his head. "No. I didn't."

My mother slept through the evening, but the deathwatch was over. Depleted, confused, annoyed by having said all my goodbyes for no good reason, I went home.

The next morning, I found her sitting up in a recliner by the window. "Oh I'm so glad you're here," she said. "I've been waiting *hours.*" She went on as she always would at doctors' offices. "Why do they *do* this? This is stupid. You wait, and wait, and then they see you for five minutes. Let's just *leave*."

I requested she be moved from the dead-end-of-hall-death-room to a room next to the nurse's station, as she would try to get up despite the bell warning on her bed, anxious to collect the keys to all her trunks and bags. She would be crying out at times, thinking I myself, her daughter, was dead.

When she finally was discharged, too weak to walk, she was brought home by ambulance—on a cumbersome archaic stretcher quite literally nearly impossible to maneuver up the three steps into her house.

As two extremely young EMS workers, sweating bullets, literally rocked the stretcher this way and that to fit it through the front door, my mother said, "Well, this is silly. Just let me get out. It's been a lovely ride but it would be easier...."

She was in the best of spirits, if she'd been off on a canoe ride and was pulling up to the dock.

After the rocking-cumbersome-stretcher ordeal, once the stricken young EMS kids had left, and my mother was settled back into her hospital bed, she said: "Well as much as I love vacations, it's always nice to be back home. But that was such *fun!*"

Such fun.

Sometimes when I visited, she would be sitting up in bed, as she had to now for twenty minutes after eating to avoid the aspiration again, despite the now painful open bedsores on her tailbone. "Well, this is such fun," she could still say, though her exuberance now weakened. She could fold her hands over her blanket. "This is a nice spot."

I welcomed this reprieve as I would her more delightful hallucinations, of "cute little chicks" scurrying around on her bureau, or the tiny child dressed all in blue: "Well, he's right there," she'd giggle, pointing to where she saw the child floating over my head. But if my mother were in her right mind, if she knew her true state—if, a month or so later, she could have understood that the "big heavy shoe" was actually her left gangrenous foot—she might have preferred being taken by the aspiration pneumonia, when perhaps she would have gone swiftly but gently, from gradual organ failure. In her last months, I too could wish she had been able to go before this withering, this near actual *desiccation*, this horrendous dawdling physical and mental decline. Because on bad days, when the delightful had taken flight like the raucous black crows from her cherry trees, she increasingly would be left not paranoid, but utterly, unwaveringly, bereft.

One day, I arrived to find Chandice had parked her wheelchair in front of her bedroom window. My mother now spent a good part of her days like this, staring out the window, even though it was December and there were no window boxes. Only a sheen of ice on the railing. She no longer looked at catalogues. If she did, she would flip through the same pages over and over, mechanically. Mostly she would stare.

I pulled the old rocker up beside her.

"Oh, Sandy, it's so good to *seee* you," she said in a trembling voice, on the edge of tears, as she often was now when she saw me. Then she was trying to shift, no longer able to sit comfortably anywhere, not even out in the large recliner. Not even with the bed pillows she sat on, to reliever her tailbone.

And I remember she began to cry then. "Oh, I don't know why I'm such a baby," she said.

"Mom." What could I say? "You have a right to complain."

"Well, no, so many have it much worse ..." She began to weep. The kind of tearless silent weeping she could do now, when her whole face trembled. "I don't know what I'm going to do..."

"Mom..." I tried to put my arm around her, longed to fully embrace her in a way I couldn't, feeling her fragility, her shoulder blades protruding through that matted pink sweater....

"Maybe it would just be better."

What Mom? What would be better?

"If I were to just go."

I knew then she didn't mean what this used to mean, that she had to leave the house she no longer recognized as home because she had left all her windows open.

"But if I go, then I will have to leave you."

I had to look away from her. I had to deviate from that moment. My mother was grappling with what it would mean if she really was ready to go, and I could not look at her. Until that moment, I had only ever known her to defy the inevitable. To promise to live to be 100: "Because I will so miss this Earth!"

I stared at her old desk, at the knotted wood, the irregular grain.

And I remember my response: "I will be ok."

I will be ok.

They were empty words.

Devoid of real meaning—I knew neither of us was convinced I would ok.

11

Wedged in between my mother's last emergencies before she died was my son's when he fell on the tip of a football that pushed his femur out of its socket. He was at practice, and Derek called me from the field. I'd spent the day out at my mother's, sitting with her as she sipped thickened pear juice, then watching Chandice swab out the Thick-It encrusted on the roof of my mother's mouth with a lollipop gauze. Returning from my mother's, reorienting was becoming harder and harder. Checking my boys' schoolbags for notes and cleaning out their lunch boxes, I could be waking from a dream—the real was still the vivid of my mother swilling water to rinse out her mouth into the plastic basin Chandice held beneath her chin. In another month, it would be my mother back in emergency, this time for a gangrenous infection, and I would sit at her beside as she imagined we were going on trip and would ask me if I had the keys to all our trunks.

There was this mental space I sought out evenings now, where I could retreat into a calm, one however momentary, as every summer up at the lake when I'd try to get up to have my coffee on the dock, before the first water bugs cast their rings. That space was relegated to one small recess of my brain where I abandoned the hard thinking to drinking. I'd just filled my wine glass when I got Derek's text: "Lucas is hurt."

Owen, thankfully, had quit football, and I wished Lucas didn't still play, but he had such a passion for the game. Though I'd worried far more about concussions than falling on the tip of a football. A most perfect storm.

Derek was then calling me. "You have to come."

I would not know how badly Lucas was hurt until I got to the field. He'd refused to go in an ambulance or to leave for the hospital without me. One of the coaches, coincidently and conveniently, was an orthopedist, and phoned ahead to a colleague at the hospital. By the time I arrived at the field, the coach had already helped to lift Lucas, in the position he fell with one leg cocked, into the back of my husband's car. Owen was in tow, and once again, we all piled into the car as we had when it was for my mother's hip, though this time it was for my ten year old's.

At the hospital, Lucas was sedated long enough for them to snap his femur back in place, but then an X-ray showed there was tissue trapped in the socket; he would have to have surgery in the morning. I listened as the doctor explained how he would clean off the ball before replacing it back in the socket. I knew this kind of talk from my mother's hip surgery. In another hospital, I'd listened to another orthopedist, who explained after her own fall, that the femoral head and upper femur would have to be replaced, using his fist to show how it would fit into the socket of his palm—a "partial" replacement which six months later would fail, and she would have the surgery again, this time a full replacement.

I already knew about hips.

How did this happen to my *son*?

The difference between these emergencies for my mother and for my child was, with my mother there was always a kind of friction between us, her at once needing me and resisting that need: "I don't want to be a burden." Being there for my son was friction*less*. His needing of me was a clear groping up out of his own terror, reaching for me as he always had: "Mommy, Mommy, Mommy, Mommy," he chanted a good part of that night, as I lay beside him in his hospital bed, careful not to snare his IV lines. I brushed his hair back off his forehead, hoping to lull him to sleep. Other times, I would have reveled in this physical closeness. When I could examine him like I used to when he was a baby, inspecting his ears, fingering that secret place on his scalp where I knew he had a birthmark. When the needing was more simply satisfied, when an embrace was enough to soothe—when the groping was him reaching up to be held after tripping on the stairs and banging his chin. Back then, his needing of me had substantiated me as his mother. Now, when I was truly needed most, I felt far more inadequate as a mother than I had ever felt as a daughter.

The next morning, after getting Owen off to school, Derek joined me in pre-op, where we flanked our ordinarily vivacious ten year old now diminished in a hospital bed, quite literally shaking with fear. We watched as masked attendants wheeled him away, leaving between us this vacuous space where the bed had been; we were left to each other in a way we hadn't been in months. And in this leaving, we were drawn together tightly, newly laced—taut in the moment, a crisis we both were equally invested in.

Otherwise, in those final months of my mother's life, Derek was my sounding board for my own crises, for all the hard choices I was making for my mother, from hiring aides to forgoing amputation of her gangrenous leg, and toward the end, hiring then firing hospice. I was a vortex of distractions, trying to remember ortho appointments and teacher conferences in between Chandice's steady stream of texts reminding me to buy more gloves, Depends, or my mother's latest fleeting favorite, pear juice or pudding. At dinner Derek might tell me about his own crises at work, and I wonder how well he saw through my thin veil of attention, as I could about my boys; whether they wondered how well I was listening when I'd pick them up from after-school care and they could chatter on about learning to make an origami swan or smoke to billow from a test tube. Which I was, listening. Though, at times it was a straining to hear them over the hum, at times real clangor, of my own thoughts.

Despite my preoccupation, Derek remained steadfast at the outer bands of my vorticity. Although he did not condone my smoking any more than my nightly bottle of wine, as a kind of joke that Christmas, he would give me a silver '70s lighter in my stocking, for those nights I snuck my cigarettes out on the front porch (as well as a camping cushion for when I sat out in the snow wrapped in a blanket). He regularly, discretely, emptied the butts from the old flowerpot. On the day my mother died, he would remind me to drive home slowly, knowing I easily could have careened off the road. That same night when I commenced my moaning, he would drive me to psychiatric emergency on the advice of my priest. Instead of admitting me, they would send me home with a diagnosis of "grieving." The following day he would get the boys off to school while I stayed in bed, wailing into my mother's balled-up matted pink sweater, inhaling the last of her.

What perhaps was harder for him to understand was the nature of my relationship with my mother: "It's like she's *inside* you," Derek railed at me one summer after we returned from a week in New Hampshire. I don't remember what prompted this comment, though while away, I probably had come to my mother's defense; rather, my own take on what otherwise sounded like criticism, but what was more my mother's usual—and yes, at times *incessant*—editorializing. We rented so many different houses over the years, I can confuse their layouts, which house had that steep hill down to the lake, the beds whose springs had worn through the mattresses. But every house, no matter how big could wind up too small, all of us inevitably left to congregate in one room, on uncomfortable loveseats on tight screened porches.

I do remember the lake house that summer feeling particularly close, with only a small round table in the kitchen for meals. The kitchen was central to the layout, and invariably we wound up sitting at the table, the boys in their booster seats. And in the middle of it all was my *mother*, who rarely could resist expressing an opinion, even with the man I married: from how much red meat he ate (bad for his cholesterol), to what could grate on him most, his parenting, interjecting "Oh, let him go..." if Derek might be telling Lucas to put on his shoes before running outside. Or "he didn't mean to..." if he might enforce a "time out" because one or the other started some fight. Derek saw it as undermining him in front of his own children—which ultimately she *was*. But I was used to this, her interjecting her opinion as freely as she always had with me, from commenting on the shirt I wore to my choice of greasy boyfriends. I could become entangled in those very opinions that Derek longed to extricate himself from, as I could in the way she had always envisioned me in those dressing-room mirrors. But as her daughter, this was just my mother being my mother.

The irony of course, was she also expressed to me what a great father she thought Derek was. How fully invested he was in her grandsons, from the time they were colicky newborns and he'd relieve me evenings so I could escape, exhausted, to Starbucks. She admired his perseverance and patience, his whiling away countless afternoons when they were infants, walking around with them in the yard so that they could swat at low hanging branches of flowering dogwood trees, and later, standing at the end of the slide to catch them on the way down; at the lake, up early to play with them in the shallows. "He's *such* a good father," my mother would say, watching him in these moments, when maybe he didn't know he was being watched by his opinionated mother-in-law.

All the same, Derek was right. My mother, in many messy ways, *was* inside me. When my first novel came out which was about—surprise!—a mother and daughter, my mother assumed the mother was her. This pissed me off no end. Did she have so little sense of herself not to know that the mother in *Blue Glass*, Marion, was the complete opposite of her? I took particular offense at her inability to credit my imaginative ingenuity with this *fictional* creation, this entirely frightened creature, so opposite of my unafraid mother. All my mother could see was what she thought her daughter thought of her: "Is this how you see me?"

But yes, my mother was indeed inside me in the actual writing of the book—intrinsically, in the very bony matter of that fictional mother and daughter left to each other as they try to forge ahead in their lives—left to themselves in all the ways they could resist the very foundation of their bond: a rock-solid boulder of love, empathy, and need. Like me, the protagonist is an only child, and I wrote out of the complexity of that singular alliance with her mother, one intensified by an absentminded father who doesn't lose his mind, but does seem to fade away. I wholly understood this: how a mother and daughter at once could reflect and deflect each other.

But how did I get to this place with my mother? Would we have evolved into something else if circumstances had been different? If my father *were* alive? If I'd grown up with siblings, who would have been forced to share my mother's attention? And in that sharing, would my mother's large boulder have been divided more evenly, and the weight lightened as we "each" carried it off into our different directions? And my mother: how might things have been different for her, if her own mother had been more supportive of her as an artist? If she had been able to understand why her daughter might have gifted her "Night Garden" in the first place? What if my grandmother had validated her daughter in the same way my mother had always, resolutely, validated me?

I don't know the answer; there is no such unequivocal. Though in the writing of this book I can wonder. As maybe we only do wonder about our relationships with our mothers in retrospect. When despite it all, how things were or might have been, we *miss* them. I miss my mother as she missed her own. Though perhaps I miss what I had with my mother, while she missed what she didn't have: that validation, her mother never having made her feel like she was "any good" as an artist. Her father may have understood her better, at the least, have recognized that her perseverance as an artist was never a conscious choice. It was as necessitated as it was with me, what I didn't realize until that period in my life when my children were toddlers, when for the first time, I was unable to write.

Still. My mother never forgot her own mother's birthday. April 2nd could come and go, but my mother never failed to recall it: "Yesterday was Mother's *birthday!*" I don't remember her ever once recalling her father's birthday.

I stayed in the hospital with Lucas for several days, as I hadn't since he was born when I was recovering from my C-section. Mornings, I would wake to a dry mouth and remember I'd forgotten to brush my teeth the night before. On my way downstairs to line up for coffee along with nurses and doctors returning to their shifts, I would pass the chapel. I dislike hospital chapels, how they mimic the holy, with fake stained-glass windows, and generic chairs you'd find in hotel conference rooms. I was used to the old stone church of my childhood, then the cathedrals when I lived in New York City, that scent of stone and wood, not antiseptic and talcum powder. In New Mexico, my mother and I visited the old adobe churches; entering their cool shadowy recesses was like moving closer to some core, as if God resided not in the heavens but inside the earth. Together we sketched these old buildings, with their stark weathered crosses, and when I'd return to the same places with my family after she died, my boys would light candles for her in Santuario Chimayo, the church of healing, where visitors knelt beside the round pit to collect the holy dirt. Where my mother and I had sat in one of the old worn pews, admiring the brilliant reds and greens of the painted altar.

One day, I did stop in the hospital chapel. By then Lucas had been fitted with a brace to stabilize his hip, from the waist down to his knee, and started physical therapy. I'd been on the phone coordinating home schooling for six weeks, a wheelchair rental, and home PT sessions. He already had learned how to get up on a walker, and I'd followed behind his tiny frame, as I had with my mother after her own hip surgeries—in a hospital gown like I'd only seen my mother wear, and I closed it around his small bottom. But on this day, he had gotten up on crutches for the first time, to walk up three steps, across a little bridge, and down again. It reminded me of the climbing toys on all the playgrounds we'd gone to when he was little, when he was fearless, hanging from monkey bars, clambering up steep, winding slides, crossing shaky rope ladders. Now he cried at the prospect of putting one foot in front of the other, in an agony equal parts pain and effort. The physical therapist seemed unmoved by his agony, either because she was used to this, children carrying on, or because my son was carrying on more than she thought was necessary. Either way, I felt sidelined; unlike at playgrounds, it was not my role to step in and take his hand when he was suddenly afraid halfway across that ladder, or to help him reach for another rung. I was rendered as helpless as I had been lying beside him, trying to soothe him before his surgery.

This hospital chapel actually had small pews, and I was able to kneel at a railing. I'd grown up kneeling in church, beside my mother, who would cradle her face in her hands. Despite all my Sunday school and confirmation classes, it was in watching my mother kneel and pray where my own faith was solidified. "Remember you can always get down on your knees and pray," she had told me all my life. When things might be going wrong, when life could feel like too much, this was her advice to me. And when my mother knelt and prayed in church, cradling her face like that, I'd wonder what exactly she was praying so hard about. Whether it was ever for any one thing—for my father when he went into the nursing home; for my sister back when she was dying; for me to find someone to marry so that she would know I was taken care of before she died. Or whether it was less actual supplication than a surrendering. A letting go of trying to keep up the momentum, of trying to swim that straight line across the bay, when inevitably she would start curving out to sea. When up at the lake, when she no longer had the energy to keep up the momentum, she would float on her back to gaze up at the sky.

I cradled my face into my hands. I prayed my son was old enough to believe in something bigger than me.

12

After the bout with pneumonia, one day, the visiting nurse called to tell me my mother had an open sore on her foot. Sores were not new. She'd first developed a blackened bedsore on her left side, where her artificial hip was beginning to protrude, and then of course, there was the issue of her raw tailbone. This sore however, was badly infected, and the nurse told me I needed to drive out immediately, to take her to the wound center at the hospital.

The infection turned out to be a result of completely blocked femoral arteries—the doctor could not find a pulse in either one; there was barely any blood flow to her extremities.

Now on a pureed diet from the stroke, my mother was a skeleton masked by brittle skin, devoid of muscle mass and fat. There was no more battle of wills. On the hospital bed, my mother lay flat on her back, staring up at the ceiling, listening. She listened to me as I shrilled at the too-young resident who said my mother would need to have her leg amputated. "You don't amputate on a 96-year-old!" *You imbecile!*

It was the wound doctor who came up with a more humane and realistic plan, pulling me away from my mother, to talk to me calmly; they would keep her for five days on IV antibiotics, then send her home with regular prescription of oral ones—which at most would slow the progression before something else finally might take her, if not the gangrene.

And in the hospital, her doctor had been frank with me. "It *will* progress."

Prognosis: if nothing else, the gangrene would take her.

The gangrene would spread up to her left knee, and similar charcoal tones would emerge on her other leg. And as hard as we tried to keep her hydrated, it was becoming more and more difficult for the technician to draw blood for her testing of Coumadin levels. Levels that fluctuated wildly, due to the powerful antibiotics she was on to keep the gangrene infection at bay.

Most visits now were about helping Chandice as much as I could; to change the dressings on bedsores; to roll my mother toward me; to reassure her that she was not falling, while she clung to the railing of her hospital bed. Rarely did my visits coincide with her nurse who came in four times a week, to change her leg dressings. Otherwise, her gangrenous leg below the knee was always neatly bandaged —concealed. I had been blessed with not having to see its actual progression.

But one week, I arrived at the same time as the nurse. "Well it's good you're here," he said, a small elf-like man with square-rimmed glasses. He snapped on latex gloves. "So you can see exactly what is going on."

Exactly what is going on.

I'd planned on leaving the room, what I realized was not only cowardly but neglectful; I was her *daughter*. And as her daughter, he expected me to stay.

He began to cut up the length of the bandages with small metal scissors. Gently unwrapping the packaged leg.

And there it was: the toes. Black flesh of her big toe

hanging off in a strip. The toenails, milky-white against blackened skin, at odd angles as if glued on sloppily by a child. Opaque like the dried sand crabs we used to collect along the beach. When we were always searching for the imperfect, of far more interest to us, in their surprising shapes.

No perfection here. I longed for perfect shells.

The charcoal of her toes extended up the foot. Up her leg. To her knee. Speckled, tar-like.

He seemed pleased. "It's progressed a bit, but not too bad."

Not too bad.

Chandice snapped on gloves as well. She was used to this, helping the nurse. There was a method and a rhythm to this wound re-dressing; she held up the leg so the nurse could cleanse the blackened heel with saline solution.

I sat stone still in my mother's wooden rocker.

The light was acutely bright coming in the windows reflected off the frozen snow piled on my mother's deck. Icy light, garish. Brazen. On the blackened heel.

He began to apply the anti-fungal meds that effectively could dry up the sores if not heal them.

My mother began to scream.

"*This* is new," the nurse said—evidently, my mother did not usually scream during a change in dressings.

And he was the most careful of nurses, though my mother was not always blessed with the same careful nurse. The previous one had not followed directives in the chart to not use gauze; gauze becomes embedded in the sores and then must be carefully peeled away without peeling off the skin. The pain of peeling even dead skin....

I wanted to look away. Out at the bare crooked cherry trees of her woods. But in their crookedness, contortion, I only saw reflected agony. I made myself stay in this moment. With my mother. I rubbed her shoulder. I told her it was almost over. I lied to her as I had to my child the night before Lucas had surgery about there being nothing for him to be afraid of, even though I was rocked by my own fear.

"Don't," she said. "Don't touch me. I'm done, done, *done!*"

I pulled my hand away, burrowed it into my lap.

The nurse took out a disposable paper ruler. To measure the blackness. The blackened.

He applied the preferred nonstick plastic-coated Telfa pads. He arranged them carefully, a well-orchestrated patchwork, around her foot, toes and lower leg, then wrapped it all securely with the rolled gauze.

And my mother: exhausted, she fell into a deep sleep, mouth open. Breathing hard.

He peeled off his gloves. "We may be getting there."

Meaning needing to administer morphine before dressing changes.

The morphine, until needed. The was a little bottle with the tiny syringe, in the sealed emergency box left in the fridge from hospice before I fired them after they refused to treat the leg beyond the superficial of saline cleansings, opting to skip the antifungal meds which at least slowed the *progress of the blackened.*

"Do you understand that she is dying?" the hospice nurse had asked me, when I'd called her out from my mother's bedroom into the living room, to confront her. She sat perched on my mother's couch, asking this with the same weightiness of my therapist, when he would try to elucidate some truth for me I was denying. Like the fact that, if my mother was in her right mind, she would be worried about me. As much as she might in the past have wished for others to care for me, now she would want to see me taking care of myself.

But this was not my therapist. And as much as I was still having trouble facing up to the fact that I was going to lose my mother, I was not stupid to this truth. When I imagine this well-intentioned being, she is faceless. But I remember her stance—the way she sat perched there on the edge of the couch, my mother's throw pillows at odd angles behind her. One was a pillow my mother made, back when I was a child, when that's what mothers did, crewel work. The pillow whose stitches I would examine after she died, as I would the haphazard ones in an old curtain she'd hemmed for the bathroom. When I'd bask in that intimacy of the hand-sewn. Different from her paintings, more private somehow, in that way our minds can wander inward when caught up in the repetitive of stitching, the basting of a hem.

The nurse had a stack of papers in her lap. She folded her hands over it. "You know she's not going to get better."

She shifted her feet just enough for the heal of one shoe to screech against the other.

"I'm not an imbecile!" I yelled.

Chandice frowned deeply. I know how she felt about the morphine–she'd been down this road before. Morphine she knew would not give my mother rest. Only rocket her off into a mental state of true wailing, not from pain but from utter disorientation. Staring, rocking...no peace. None.

"Let's see how it goes next time," the nurse said to me. "Then you can let me know what you want to do."

What I want to do.

Before he left, he helped Chandice to roll my mother onto her side, to relieve that pressure on her tailbone.

My mother closed her eyes, lay with her hands folded up near her chin. She actually looked comfortable which most of the time she wasn't.

I put down the side rail so I could reach her, to stroke her hair, her face, barely touching, so afraid of hurting her. The way I'd sat by what I thought was her deathbed in the hospital, memorizing her: the moles, the fine hairs on her chin, the wisps of white hair, the birthmark on her forehead she'd always referred to as a "black mark" against her.

I rested my head beside hers and closed my own eyes. We lay like that, in kind of abeyance, until she asked, "So where did we meet?"

I thought about how to answer. Or not.

"At birth."

She looked at me. "What?"

"We met when you birthed me. At my C-section."

Her stomach began to shake under her blanket, as a weak laugh welled up. Then she said, "You should write a book. You really should."

A book. The best laugh of all.

She closed her eyes again.

"I'm cold," she muttered, from that halfway place between wakefulness and sleep.

I pulled the blankets up to her chin, and she reached one hand out from beneath the fleece throw. Feeling around for me, she said, "You're a very satisfying daughter."

I placed my hand on top of her cold one.

I didn't wake her to say goodbye. I dared not even kiss her on her forehead. Because this appeared to be real sleep —often she lay there, not really sleeping, maybe stressing about whether she was up for the "trip," or what to do with "all her houses," and she was so tired from moving from place to place to place... "I'm so tired, tired, tired of all this traveling, I just want to go *home*!"

She slept.

I was relieved.

Relieved.

Later, when I called her, she would be crying. "I heard you were here. And I missed seeing you. Why didn't you wake me? Sandy, I don't want to miss *seeing* you!"

13

One night, Chandice called to tell me water was pooling out from under the cellar door into the hall.

At the *top* of the stairs.

She was afraid to open the door, as if expecting a tidal wave. "You need to call a plumber."

I called the same plumber I'd found in the phone book, and when he opened the door, he was met with a horrific site: the entire stairwell had mushroomed huge blooms of mold. The expansion tank on the water heater was leaking, and in the space of 48 hours, a highly toxic mold had propagated freely throughout the now tropical steamy cellar. The insurance adjuster would tell me that he had not seen anything like it since Hurricane Sandy. No pun intended.

My mother would not die for another six weeks, and the actual deed to the house would not be turned over into my name for another year. But in that period of true house disaster, I was indoctrinated into real ownership. My mother's "happy house" was turned inside out. Not only would all the insulation and sheetrock be ripped out in the stairwell—in the wall to Chandice's bedroom—but the environmental tester would measure even higher mold counts in my mother's attic, where evidently, the chimney had been leaking for decades. Equally high counts would be found in the gallery outside my mother's studio, cursed with a flat roof that collected rainwater—the ceiling there too, would be ripped out.

So toward the very end of my mother's life, there would be anything but peace and quiet. There would the demolition of ceilings and walls, the roar of a cement mixer to poor a concrete floor into the bowels of a cellar with an otherwise sand-and-dirt floor these past one hundred years. Masons would be up on the roof, dismantling the crumbling chimney. On those days when I wasn't on the phone to my mother's doctors, about her wildly fluctuating Coumadin levels, the spread of the gangrene up her leg, and antibiotics for her bedsores, I was on the phone with not only the insurance company, but with mold remediators, masons, contractors, plumbers, and painters.

All of this happened towards the end of February, when there was still a foot of old snow on the ground. My mother by then was quite literally on her deathbed—the hospital one moved into her bedroom. Thankfully, her room was located in a part of the house away from the moldy basement.

In those last weeks, if my mother woke before I got back on the road to drive home, it was a brief rising to the surface, a lingering there only long enough to sink back under; oblivious to the demolition around her, of her happy house quaking with its own grief.

Before this melding of the hours, of day into night, occasionally, my mother would tell me about her dreams: a feeling of being in love, though she didn't know who with. Or one of herself having been abandoned, to wander a grey landscape. Dreams she wanted to dream more of, others she was relieved to wake from.

Now I did not know if she dreamt at all.

What I did know was often people sleep most of the day months before they actually die. That was my mother. I would drive out to see her, and she would sleep most of time I was there, except one day, she was sitting up when I arrived.

She was only sitting up because she had just eaten, and Chandice had elevated the head of her bed. Meals which were at odd times now, and that morning, Chandice said she'd been up since five. She had just finished spoon-feeding my mother applesauce mixed with a little yogurt, what she also might eat for dinner, her appetite waning.

I'd bought her sunflowers, fresh ones as I did now every week. After filling a vase with water, I set them on her bureau. If things had been as they'd always been, she would have exclaimed "Oh, how *gorgeous*!" and asked me to put them on a glass plate so not to leave a ring. But within the space of the few minutes I'd left to inspect the house renovations, she'd drifted back to sleep, her mouth hanging open.

"Look what I brought you," I said loudly, wanting, *needing* her to wake up.

She opened her eyes long enough to glimpse the flowers. "Oh...."

I felt then a petulant disappointment wash over me, the child ignored by her mother.

She closed her eyes again, but then asked, "You ok?"

"I'm ok," I said, trying, failing, to hide my hurt. Which had nothing finally to do with the flowers.

"You don't sound ok."

I couldn't speak.

At my silence she opened her eyes, glassy, one eye a slit. "You don't need to worry about me," she said. "I don't want to worry about you worrying about me."

I pulled up the rocker next to her bed. "And I don't want to worry about you worrying about me worrying about you."

A laugh rippled through us both before dissipating like a sudden breeze.

There was a loud bang from the other side of the house. They were installing new sheetrock to the wall of the cellar stairs.

"Thunder," she said. "It's going to rain."

After the twenty minutes, she was tired, and Chandice came in to lower the head of her bed.

Donning gloves, I helped her to change my mother's bandages on the open sores as I regularly did now, on both hips, on her tailbone.

We rolled her to one side so that she clung to the bed rail. Afraid of falling.

We settled her legs onto a pillow to support her bandaged gangrenous one.

But that railing. She wouldn't let go.

"It's ok, Mom. You're not going to fall."

"Let her be," Chandice whispered. "It makes her feel safer."

My mother clung. Shaky hands, a tangle of tiny veins.

Chandice, taking up the basin from rinsing her mouth of the Thick-It, left the room.

"So..." My mother just looked at me for a moment, as if orienting herself. "Meeting anyone new?"

She was placing me, again, back in another time and place.

"No. Same old, same old."

"Well." She closed her eyes, as hard as she had tried to keep them open. As if they were weighted down. "Go out and live it up. Don't be like me."

Don't be like me.

She loosened the grip on the railing. To run her fingers back and forth along the cold metal, as if feeling her way through some dark. She reached out a hand.

I thought toward me. I grasped it.

She opened her eyes. "Oh." She laughed a little. "I

thought you were the cat." She patted my hand. "But I love, love, love *love* you so much."

This was not new. In those last months, we chanted this regularly to each other, our own private prayer. *I love you so so so much.*

Then she said, "I want to buy you something really special. What do you want for your birthday?"

She could obsess now about my birthday. I did not want to tell her how it had already passed, just that February. Before she was sleeping all the time, I'd made the mistake of showing her a new handbag, and she'd grabbed it from me, begging me to let her give it to me for my birthday: "Oh, but please. I want to give this to you for your *birthday*!" So the handbag I'd bought for myself became my birthday present to me which she forgot all about within five minutes of her gifting it.

Now she said, her attention fully trained on me, "Sandy. What can I give you that's really special?"

I resisted smoothing her white hair off her forehead as I had my son's messy bangs when I'd tried to soothe Lucas in the hospital. He was back in school by then, though still on crutches. And I wanted to tell her about what an ordeal it had been, how I understood now how we can worry obsessively over our children, as she still could worry over me.

She pushed my hand away as if she didn't want me to muss her hair. But maybe it was more than that. Like it was with my son now. Who didn't want me pitying him, as much as he did, very much, want Mommy.

She slid her hands back and forth restlessly along the railing. "I don't know how much longer I can hold on…" And I was reminded of the times she would cry out that she couldn't take any more of it. *Any of it.*

So I took this opportunity to assure her: "It's ok to let go."

She stared at me. "It is?"

"You don't have to keep holding on, Mom."

"But I don't want to fall. Oh no, I'm falling..." She readjusted her grip on the railing, and I realized this moment was not about the real letting go.

She was panicked.

"You can let go of the railing Mom, it's ok. You're not falling."

"No?"

"No."

"Because I'm so tired from holding on..." she started to cry that tearless cry.

"Mom." I placed my hand over hers. "Let go. I won't let you fall..."

Gradually she loosened her grip. I took her hand. I rubbed it. Ice cold from gripping the cold metal rail.

"See?"

She calmed down.

And I reminded her that she was lying in bed.

"I am?"

Yes you're in bed and you're not falling.

"I hope not, because if I fall there might be frogs jumping all over me."

Her mouth fell back open. She drifted back to sleep. Back under.

From her windows, I could see men tossing all the contents of my mother's cellar out into the yard. They appeared other worldly, the white of their Hazmat suits a shining glory against the gray of old snow. I really didn't know what was down in that cellar until it was all being thrown outside: my old toy cart with the orange wheels that my father used to wheel himself around on to weed our front walk; bent and rusted shovels and saws; flowerpots and cracked hanging plastic planters; my mother's favorite lounge chair, its blue now a muted moldy green. And in this watching of the other worldly, in this gazing as into an aquarium at the distorted and magnified,

I felt disembodied. As if I wasn't sitting there beside my mother who slept the groundless sleep of the dying, oblivious to the destruction around her. As if I were entirely alone. Already abandoned.

14

Except for the day when she actually died, my mother no longer called me.

I don't remember exactly when she stopped calling me—when exactly she forgot my phone number, or even to look for it where I'd written it under that tile. When she forgot where I lived at all; that I'm 30-plus years out of college; that she has two grandchildren. That I no longer am taking "classes" and having "boyfriends," or need to plan ahead to when I'll be having "babies."

But I still would call her, and Chandice would hold the phone to her ear.

"You sound down," my mother said.

I was calling her one evening. Just after having seen her. Knowing she would already not remember seeing me.

She had always been able to hear sadness in my voice.

"What is it, Sandy?"

And then I was crying. I cried on the phone to my mother who was suddenly, fully, my mom—swiftly oriented by her daughter's sadness. I like to think that in that moment, she knew exactly where she was. She knew she was in her bedroom of the house she'd lived in for 30 years. That she recognized the desk opposite her bed. Maybe even the painting above her bureau. Her own painting. An abstract, of the ocean. One that resonated. Of her. Of my mom.

"Oh, Honey Bun," she said. "I hate to hear you this way..."

I cried and cried to her. Because in her own reorientation, I lost my own.

And because, unlike in the past, I could not tell her what was wrong. What had been going on all around her, how her happy house seemed to be caving in, unable to bear its own weight any more than I could my compounded griefs—I could not tell her about her grandson who had been confined to a wheelchair as only she had been. Of how he was now back in school but anxious and afraid that something else bad was going to happen to him. How in the hospital he'd screamed with the effort of it all, a child bent over his own little walker, as I'd only ever seen my mother. How, between all the heartaches of the people I loved most, I was finding it hard to breathe. To rise to my own surface, to find those little pockets of air.

And I could not tell her the reason I finally couldn't stop crying. Because having, if only for a moment, her *back,* so fully as my mom, was utterly wrenching. Devastating.

As if we were still what we'd always been.

Which we were not.

I cried and cried and cried.

"Oh Honey, please don't," she pleaded, as only a mother can plead, when her child is hurting and she doesn't know how to help. "This too will pass," she said. "There's the good then the bad, then the good..."

I don't remember where I was for this call. But I remember it as if I'd collapsed to my knees as I would on the day she died. "I'm okay."

And then she was expressing some discomfort, and I knew she needed rotating in her bed. "I'm going to have to go," she said, and I heard Chandice coming in to check on her.

We hung up.

I took a long bath. I submerged my head enough so that I could hear the water. The way I imagined dolphins can hear; intelligent creatures, but perhaps better than us in communicating through the sensory. And I listened.

15

The last phone call from my mother was on the morning of April 15th, 2015, when she called to tell me this: "Sandy, I'm dying."

I knew Chandice was holding the phone for my mother, as she was too weak to hold it herself.

Chandice had texted me earlier that my mother had woken up unable to move.

My mother told Chandice to call me.

Call Sandy.

I have no memory of where I was when I answered the phone. But when I envision myself, I am standing in the hallway of the house I grew up in. Looking at the vines of tiny blue flowers of the wallpaper going up the staircase. The old grandfather clock ticking in the background, that gentle beat of the brass pendulum. After my mother died, I often dreamt of myself back in that house, standing in that hall, taking that last phone call from my mother.

I laughed a little; it struck me as nonsensical. "How can you know you're dying?"

She took a short shallow breath. As if short of breath. "I just know."

My mother and I then told each other how much we

loved each other. I would not remember this, but later, Chandice would assure me that this was how our last phone conversation went.

Then I asked to talk to Chandice.

I asked Chandice what she thought. Whether this was another hallucination, whether this was real, whether I needed to drive out there.

This determined, opinionated woman sounded unsure: "I don't know..."

She was crying. Once again I was shocked by my own terror at losing my mother, as I had been when she fell and almost bled out, and then again, when I'd expected she'd succumb to the aspiration pneumonia. Now she was 96, clearly dying long before this last day, and I still worried something could happen to her.

Then this: Chandice told me that my mother had outstretched her hand to thank her for all she'd done. The clarity of this gesture still astonishes me. My mother, who for months had been in and out of excruciating dementia, who at times could berate and call Chandice names, suddenly understood with extraordinary clarity the reality of this woman: without Chandice, she would not have been able to die in her own home.

I called my priest, knowing she would be able to find me someone from the parish to take care of the boys. And I was on the road. Driving that stretch of highway, between those two points on a map, between my mother and me.

By the time I got there, my mother was actually sitting up, had even drunk a little pear juice, and Chandice laughed. "She had me fooled again!" she said, clearly, for the first time, trying to deceive herself about the truth of my mother. Because this was what she admired in my mother, how she rallied to life again and again. And for that brief moment, it was Chandice who had lost all reason.

But my mother's skin color had changed. She was sallow. Something Dr. Craig would remark on when she came by later that evening; when she'd open that little box from the refrigerator to take out the little bottle of morphine; when we stood around my mother's butcher's block kitchen table.

Chandice lowered the head of the hospital bed so we could roll my mother onto her side, to change out the wet chux pad, and facing me, my mother said, "Well, *someone* has a big tummy."

No doubt with all the wine, and eating whatever I could grab, now I really *did* need a girdle.

Then things took a turn. Once we settled her on her back, she went into a seizure—her eyes rolled up into her head, flickering like a mechanical doll's, and she began muttering gibberish.

She vomited black bile.

And Chandice said: "I'm sorry. She's going."

Chandice supported my mother while I cut open her nightgown covered in black bile, the only way we could get it off of her. Chandice slipped over her head what was at hand, a stained white T-shirt.

My mother had known before any of us what was happening to her. But by this time, she seemed to have forgotten what she already knew, asking, "What's wrong with me?"

You're dying.

Then my mother began to count, Chandice's eyes grew wide; she had witnessed this before with other dying clients, and believed it meant death was imminent, that they were quite literally counting their last seconds.

I believed otherwise. I believed this was my mother's way of hanging on—with, oddly enough, a clarity of mind to understand that her brain was actually beginning to shut down.

I counted with her. One, two, three, four...until she

began to weave in and out of coherency, speaking gibberish until she found a word: "Talk!"

We talked. Chandice rambled on about the cats, how Sam ate too much and was getting too big.

"Keep talking." she commanded.

As long as we talked she would not die.

I sang the song that had "inspired" her: "From a distance," the only song that came to mind because Chandice had played it for her last week, after my mother turned to her one day and said, "Inspire me." I had asked Chandice to play for her my mother's favorite old Judy Collins CDs, and when that song came on, Chandice sang along, taking my mother's hands as she lay in bed, swaying them to the music.

I did not imagine what our last moments together would really be like, a disjointed, nonsensical conversation punctuated by random words: socks, coats and half a bike.

"How can you have only half a bike?" I demanded, irritated now. I needed *to reason!*

For relief from her pressure sores, Chandice and I rolled her onto her right side, sliding a pillow under her hips for support. My mother closed her eyes. Her breaths were shallow and rapid.

"A half," she insisted.

"Where's the other half?"

Don't trying talking reason to your mother.

She thrust her fleece throw, balled in her fist, at me. "Here. Take it! The coat!"

I reached for the throw. "Ok. I have the coat."

Then she was reaching her hand out from beneath it, to anxiously slide it up and down my arm, tucking her fingers under my shirt sleeve, searchingly.

I had lost by then my own words.

And she had stopped the counting.

We continued the morphine and started the liquid

lorazepam.

She seemed to drift off to sleep around 11pm. Chandice told me to go to bed.

I refused to. I couldn't leave her side.

"This isn't how it's done," Chandice said.

This isn't how it's done.

How should it be done?

I had no idea.

So I went to bed.

16

I've never imagined myself anywhere else but at her bedside when my mother actually passed. Nor that I could possibly have fallen into such a deep sleep, that I'd be startled by Chandice, at 4:30 am, calling for me up the stairs: "Sandy!"

I stumbled out of bed, surprised by how deeply I'd slept, and ran down to my mother's room.

My mother was already gone.

I'd missed the moment. And I was furious. At Chandice.

"How could you not wake me?"

"I checked on her at three," she said, sounding baffled, and upset. "She was the same. Then I checked...now..."

We both looked at my mother. Eyes closed, her face sallow, her mouth open, drooping to one side.

This is what I remember doing, but whether or not I actually did, I really don't know: I shook my mother. I shook her, surprised that she was as languid now as a rag doll. Wake up, Mom. Wake up!

Dr. Craig returned to write out the death certificate, and Chandice called the funeral home. I climbed into that hospital bed with my mother. Chandice left us alone, shutting the door as quietly as if my mother were only sleeping.

I pulled her close to me. I gazed into her face for a long time.

I wished she would open her eyes.

I wanted her to look at me, one last time, because in those last weeks, my mother's eyes often seemed not to receive and reciprocate the seeing. The last time I'd visited before she died, that was the extent of our communication: her blinking, staring at me blankly. Me staring back, trying to penetrate the blue of her eyes. Her pupils, black moons against blue skies. Blue skies as blue as shallow pool water. And I'd been anxious to describe that blue exactly: the complex sheen of a blue-jay feather? The polychromatic blue of a dying match? The sharp blue of a crisp autumn sky? The iridescent blue of a mussel's inner shell? The mercurial blue of new snow at dawn? Because it was my mother who taught me that, how to see: "Oh look at that," she could gasp, in reverence to a muted sky. With a sweeping gesture, she would draw my attention to the way light could at once seem strained and gently filtered, excited by such paradoxes.

Now I lifted the lid of one eye. I stared at the black moon, and all I felt was her absence. I was surprised that when I let go, it fell back shut.

I would not realize until later why I had not instinctively woken up at the moment of my mother's passing. How I could I not have been jolted awake by this cataclysmic final shift between us? *How,* Mom?

Because this is how my mother would have wanted to leave me: careful not to wake her sleeping child. As careful as I was with my own sleeping children, to step away quietly.

A lawn mower started up somewhere. Miraculously, a life outside my mother's house continued.

It was dawn. There was the singing of the first birds,

and I whispered in my mother's ear, "Mom, hear the birds?"

Their song now laced with the passing of a moment. Of a life. Of my mother.

Afterword

Before I was finally admitted to the hospital, I wound up in psychiatric emergency three times, twice sent home with the diagnosis of grieving. If I was grieving, then why was it so hard for me to cry? "It's your coping mechanism," my therapist explained, because if I were to break down, it would be like in my dreams where I seemed to do my real grieving. Where I often was reduced to a weeping heap as I had been in my mother's foyer when they drove away with her body—crying *real* tears, because when I visit my mother in the hospital, they are unable to tell me what room she is in. They tell me it is my fault for not knowing, because in the dream, I don't answer when she phones to tell me where she is. In these dreams, she is hurt and angry to think I've forgotten her, and I make other phone calls, hoping someone has seen her—someone does, down at the beach: a woman who looks just like my mother. The way people could look like her after she died, in the distance, carrying themselves as only my mother had, when for an instant, there was this, the immediacy of the dreamt; when it is actually her walking toward me, in one of my father's old Oxfords over a white T-shirt, wearing her favorite soldered bangles that I can still hear ring. The beach turns to the vast dry expanse of a desert, and when she reaches me, I rest my head on her chest, surprised and frightened by the feel of her hollowed out where her breasts had been.

The first two days after I was admitted, I slept the sleep of the dying. How I imagine my mother slept in her last weeks, when her happy house was turned inside out. When her mouth went slack, and nothing could wake her. I slept the sleep of the dreamless. A truly dark sleep, the pitch-black of sinking so deep, no light can penetrate. Whenever I woke, it was to some brilliant gleam through the locked hospital windows, and I quite literally did not know if the sun was rising or setting—I slept around the clock, waking only for meals, to wade through my own fog to the cafeteria, not knowing whether to expect dinner or breakfast. "What time is it?" I'd ask, not knowing if the hall clock that said seven was seven in the morning or at night. I would wake from this pitch-black sleep as disoriented as I imagined my mother had been.

By then, my mother had already been gone almost two months, and I had done those immediate things I had to do. I had walked back into our house after driving home the day my mother died and told our sons that their Gramma was gone. Lucas was online with a friend playing Minecraft. He looked at me for a moment, then turned back to his screen. Speaking into his microphone, to this amorphous friend, he said, "My Gramma just died." As if in the saying he could understand it as real. A loss far less tangible than when his gerbil died, and he'd been able to bury it himself, marking it with his own little stones. Owen: I don't remember his reaction. But Christmas morning, he was the first to burst into tears while opening one of his ornaments, a small Santa with long skinny legs Gramma had given him. It was broken, one leg snapped off. He ran up to his room and cried in his bed for the next two hours, with Lucas then breaking down himself. I would unwrap the rest of the ornaments, all with my mother's distinctive signature on the little tags.

As to walking back into my mother's house, I first had to return to take care of the cats; unable to keep the cats because Lucas and I were allergic and because I couldn't find them a home, I had to give them up to rescue. I had stood in her foyer, averting my eyes from her bedroom—the hospital bed was gone, replaced by her own bed, and just the sight of it so neatly made with her blue comforter and throw, nearly tore back open my initial raging weeping. Chandice helped me to corral the cats into their carrier; she understood as I did that my mother would never forgive me for giving up the cats, but that it was something that needed doing for either of us to move forward. She tried to help me in all the small ways she could, like making up the bed, then remaking it with a new bed sham and new salmon-colored sheets; I quite literally could not walk into my mother's bedroom until it was altered; transformed. I would write Chandice a final check, and she would eventually pack up and return to the Bronx, though to worry over me as only my mother had.

Whenever I walked into my mother's house alone now, I moved quickly through her rooms as I had when she was alive, when I'd imagined this, the *now*, of her gone. I'd *quickly* empty her bureau drawers of the too intimate: underwear, mastectomy bras, those hateful hospital socks. I threw out enema boxes, stool softeners, Saline bottles. I donated leftover bandages and Depends, walkers and wheelchairs to the local nursing home. I did this in a terrible rush, skirting the agony of this pivotal loss. Though then there was the intimate I saved: fragmented powder compacts. Hair brushes. Her lipsticks. That old Chanel Number 5 perfume. Those *tangible* things that resurrected my mother for me in that way I ached for her as

I had as a child, for that physical closeness of her rocking me when she would sing "Silent Night." When I could put my ear to her chest and both feel and hear her beating heart.

From the funeral home, I had picked up my mother's ashes in a large plastic baggy tightly stuffed into a black plastic bin, what looked like a black office garbage pail (she would have thought it ridiculous for me to spend money on anything more ornate). The bin was presented to me by the funeral director as if he'd purchased me a gift; in a small green bag, the kind of shopping tote my mother might have saved for her catch-alls, those loose pill bottles or pocket notebooks when we went up to the lake. Back in my car, I laughed until tears were streamed down my face, at the ridiculous little bag beside me, with the gold embossed lettering. I laughed until I was crying as my mother would have laughed with me, at the sight of herself coming home to me like some nice jewelry purchased from a Macy's counter.

Once home, I sat at my dining-room table, untied the enormous baggy. I reached in and grabbed fistfuls of my mother as if I could keep her from running out between my fingers. Human ashes are like sand—all grit. Not powder. Though finally nothing like sand; so fine, the ash that spilled onto my table became ingrained in the wood.

I licked the tip of one finger—at once sour and sweet.

The taste of my mother....

The harrowing was not in the seeking.

It was in the tasting.

And in the holding—the prized find. Tiny bones I sought out that hadn't been pulverized, the artifacts of my mother; tentatively, gently, I pushed them around in my palm.

I would not actually get around to burying my mother until I was released from the hospital. I would not yet have tucked her paint brushes, her favorite drawing pens, snips of my own hair, and one of my own drawings from our summers at the lake, into her plastic urn. And I would not be able to bring myself to clean out her clothes for another three years, the too-familiar old sweaters and that pink sweater scented with her the way the air is after a summer storm. It would be another year before I would uncover those letters of longing to her father, the child's drawings, the stories of fairies and one of the moon with many rooms, when I finally could bring myself to organize a memorial service for her, and I was seeking out whatever I could find of her in her happy house. I would find that single lock of brilliant blond hair—I'd never seen the actual color of her hair, what appeared pallid in those sepia-toned crumbling photographs of her as a child. The curls pinned back from her face, with the big white bow. Holding a lock of my mother's hair from when she was a child, feeling the texture of that brilliant youthful blond, was the beginning of coming to know my mother as a whole person. The way I couldn't when she was alive, when it was her aura I knew best.

After a couple of days in the hospital, they stopped giving me whatever made me sleep around the clock. I washed what few clothes I had with me, in the communal washing machine, only to have someone insist my underwear belonged to her; "they're mine," she said, clutching my underthings to her chest, until I wrenched my panties free. I would only be there a few more days, but it would feel like weeks, and I made collect calls to my husband, wondering what my boys thought, and to my priest, from the cafeteria pay phone with a cord so short, no one could strangle themselves. I pleaded with them to convince the "they" that I was not suicidal. That I just wanted to go *home*!

I was allowed outside in the courtyard, blending into a

small group, where there was a basketball hoop with no net because someone had tried to hang themselves. One day, "they" handed out some flyer, something about how to take better care of ourselves. The "they" I remember as some amorphous being who talked to us in hushed tones carried off on the warm spring breeze, lifted up and away like the petals from the cherry blossom trees on the other side of the chain-link fence.

A girl wrapped in a long brown sweater, folded her own flyer into an airplane and shot it up angrily toward the sun. She tucked her hands far up into her large dolman sleeves and crouched against the stucco hospital wall.

I too sat back against the wall warmed by the sun but closed my eyes to the bright clear day; too searing somehow, for us all. We did not know our different stories. But we knew we were all admitted for the same reason: we were frayed. We were all painfully fragile.

Patients were discharged and admitted daily, some wailing through the night, in their sleep even after they'd been administered that same sleeping potion, and I do not remember a single name of anyone.

Not even of my roommates, one who was a psychic medium—*I kid you not.*

I've never been to a psychic medium but I did not imagine one so plain and grounded as this one, walking the halls in her practical Crocs, with her hair tied back in a single band. One of the smokers, she incessantly chewed the nicotine gum they doled out at the nurse's station, and mothered our other roommate, a young wide-eyed girl who was there because she threw a television through a window. This teenager, who liked to watch me, gaze unblinking as I changed after coming out of the shower as if I was some boring TV rerun, was happiest lying on her bed examining her acrylic nails. The only time we actually talked was when she couldn't wait to be released so that she could get fixed the one that had chipped.

The psychic would French braid our roommate's hair when again, the girl found out she was not to be discharged, and would storm back into our room to throw herself face down on her bed. The psychic soothed her by promising to French braid her hair every day until she was discharged, as long as they were both there, and since you never knew day to day whether you would be discharged, the braiding became marks on all of our mental calendars.

Because I did not care to make conversation, I would not find out she was a psychic until it was me storming back into the room in tears. Every day we would line up in the hall to be evaluated by our doctors, and again I found out they did not think I was ready to be discharged. When I asked my doctor why couldn't I go *home*, he'd said, without looking up from his clipboard, "Because. I'm not convinced you're not suicidal."

Running off in tears, was not helpful, no doubt, but the psychic understood.

I cried openly in front of the psychic and the teenager; she was sitting on the girl's bed, braiding her long stick-straight hair. The girl was clutching a stuffed emoji smiley-face pillow.

The psychic knew without my having to say anything: "It's hard, I know. I thought I was leaving yesterday."

I talked through my tears, the most I'd talked to anyone there (part of the reason, I'd learn, they had not discharged me was because I had failed to "respond" by socializing at meals and showing up for daily meetings.)

I have no memory of what I said to this psychic, though evidently—unsurprisingly—it was about losing my mother.

What I remember is her response: a simple nod. Knowingly.

For the first time, I felt like making conversation. I asked her about herself; for some reason, I imagined her in real estate or banking.

That was when she told me she was a psychic. Folding one strand of hair back over another, she said, "And...your mother has been here all along."

She nodded as she said this, as if acknowledging this to herself as well. The fact was, I'd at times felt badly about not making conversation, as she had this way of smiling sympathetically at me whenever I passed her in the hall or room. She'd been watching me I now realized. Because yes, I—rather, my mother—had been on her mind.

She then told me my mother was quite "feisty."

I could imagine that, my mother insistent, breaking into the line of other souls waiting to be heard. How she must have recognized through this otherwise ordinary motherly woman in Crocs, a way to me.

And the psychic told me she "hung out with her father mostly."

I was not surprised.

Then she looked at me. "Was there something about socks?"

It was only once I was discharged when I would wonder if this wasn't about when she was dying and handing me imaginary socks.

And as casually as if noting the obvious she said: "Well, anyway, she just wants to thank you. For everything you've done."

For everything I've done.

On the day she died, it was Chandice whom my mother thanked.

But now I was the one she was straining to reach.

Because even here, in this murky suspension between the then and now, I was this:

I was my mother's daughter.

Author's Note

As a novelist writing a memoir, at times I have compressed events and embroidered character and dialogue. But in my recall and retelling, any resorting to fictional devices is not about fabrication. It is about bringing into high relief the heart of this story–the lived emotive truth of one mother and daughter and those central to them. To protect the privacy of individuals, some names and characteristics have been changed.

About the Author

Sandra Tyler is the athor of **BLUE GLASS**, a *New York Times Notable Book of the Year*, and **AFTER LYDIA**, both published by *Harcourt Brace*. She earned her BA from Amherst College, and her MFA in creative writing from Columbia University. She has taught creative writing at Columbia University, NY; Wesleyan University, CT; Manhattanville College, NY. She is the editor-in-chief and founder of the premier online literary and fine art magazine, **The Woven Tale Press**.

www.ingramcontent.com/pod-product-compliance
Lightning Source LLC
LaVergne TN
LVHW040140100425
808242LV00011B/96/J